CYBERNAUTS AWAKE!

GS Misc 569

CYBERNAUTS AWAKE!

Ethical and Spiritual Implications
of Computers, Information
Technology and the Internet

CHURCH HOUSE
PUBLISHING

Church House Publishing
Church House
Great Smith Street
London
SW1P 3NZ

ISBN 0 7151 6586 0

Published 1999 for the Board for Social Responsibility of the Church of England by Church House Publishing.

This report has only the authority of the working group that produced it. It has been approved by the Board for Social Responsibility.

Acknowledgements

Biblical passages are reproduced from:

The Revised Standard Version (RSV), copyright 1946, 1952, © 1971, 1873 by the Division of Christian Education of the National Council of the Churches of Christ in the USA.

The *New English Bible* (NEB) copyright © Oxford University Press and Cambridge University Press 1961, 1970.

Cover design by Jonathan Richards, Image-On Artworks

Printed in England by Halstan & Co. Ltd

Contents

Members of the Working Party

Professor Derek Burke (Chair of the working party), member of the Science, Medicine and Technology Committee; former Vice-Chancellor of the University of East Anglia; specialist advisor to the House of Commons Science and Technology Select Committee

Christine Crosbie (Secretary to the working party)

Mr Nicholas Beale, member of the Worshipful Company of Information Technologists

Ms Theresa Byrne, Roman Catholic Bishops' Conference of England and Wales: Secretary to the Committee for the World of Work and the Committee for Public Life

Dr Dave Leal, Lecturer in Philosophy and Moral Theology, Regent's Park College, University of Oxford

Professor Simon Peyton Jones, former professor of Computing Science at the University of Glasgow

Professor John Pickering, Professor of Business Strategy at the University of Bath

Dr David Pullinger, e-commerce consultant; Senior Vice President of IQ Port Ltd; Visiting Professor at Middlesex University; former Electronic Publisher of *Nature*; former Director of the Society, Religion and Technology Project of the Church of Scotland

Professor Harold Thimbleby, Director of Research at the School of Computing Science, Middlesex University

Preface

The Church of England Board for Social Responsibility has the task of helping the Church to engage in critical debate with contemporary society. Developments in Information Technology have changed our lives in numerous ways. As the twentieth century draws to a close there can be little doubt that we have only just begun to appreciate the extent to which our social, economic and cultural life is being transformed. The board's Science, Medicine and Technology Committee proposed in 1996 that the board should commission a working party to set out some of the ethical and spiritual implications of these extraordinary developments. We are grateful to Professor Derek Burke and his colleagues for the hard work that they have put into the task of producing this report.

Cybernauts Awake! is not the sort of title usually associated with the report of a working party commissioned by the Church. The style of the report is deliberately informal. It does not seek to present an official Church view. Rather, it tries to set out as clearly and fairly as possible some of the issues that we all need to be thinking about. It will have served its purpose if it encourages its readers to think – particularly if they read it on the Internet!

✠ *Richard Oxon*

Chairman

Church of England Board for Social Responsibility

Introduction

There is an extraordinary transformation taking place in society. Cyberspace, for many years the preserve of computer specialists, is becoming the most important means of communication. Some banks will only take new customers over the Internet. Long-established firms are dwarfed in value by start-up companies doing e-commerce. The Internet plays a key role in major political events from the downfall of President Suharto to the impeachment of President Clinton. Serbia jams Nato's web site. People thousands of miles away meet over the Internet, marry and ultimately have children. This new medium of communication is coming in like a flood, and all of us from the 5-year-old to the 85-year-old are being drawn in. There are tremendous opportunities for businesses, for charities, public bodies, churches and for individuals. More than ever before, cyberspace allows computers to become 'dream machines'. But every dream has its dark side. What about the drawbacks? Will our children grow up to become zombies, always sitting in front of a screen? What about the loss of jobs, the invasion of privacy, the pornography?

One thing is certain: we shall not be able to stop the growth of this new technology, even if we wanted to. It is far too helpful, too fascinating and too much fun for that. It is certain too that this new technology, like any other, is inherently neither wholly good nor wholly bad, but neither is it neutral; for it is changing the way we work, play, perhaps the way we think about ourselves and each other, and crucially, the way we relate to each other.

It is exactly because we are fascinated by this new technology and also aware of its ability to change our lives that we have written this book. We don't have many answers, but we hope that we have raised some important questions, and advanced the debate. We hope too that this book will be read both by the near beginner and by the expert, because this is not another 'how to' book, but a 'what if' book, a book to which all can respond.

Much has been written about the impact of information technology and the Internet on us as human beings and the society we live in. Most of this has been written from a secular perspective, and much less discusses what effect this new technology might have on our spiritual lives. Our purpose in writing this book is to approach these questions from a specifically Christian perspective, but we believe that what we have written will be of interest to all who care about our society and where it is going, and we have consciously written with them in mind as well.

The project had its origin in the Science, Medicine and Technology Committee of the Board for Social Responsibility of the Church of England, who have been supportive throughout, and we owe much to its secretary, David Skidmore, and our secretaries, Christine Crosbie, Margaret Jeffery and Claire Foster. We hope you enjoy it.

1

Dream Machines

Every now and again something happens to us that lets us dream new dreams. The invention of the printing press, the European discovery of America, the industrial revolution, the emergence of democracy, going to the moon, the fall of the Berlin Wall . . . we can all think of examples. The interesting thing about all these changes is that, as well as their immediate practical impact, they each opened up new visions of what we have in us to be, or do. Each, too, has its dark side; dreams are not unequivocally 'good' or 'bad' in a simple way.

Most people would agree that the impact of computers, and the programs that run on them, what we call information technology (IT), is similarly profound – they are truly dream machines. We are probably most aware of the immediate practical effects, such as word processors and mobile phones, but computers are willy-nilly changing the society we live in, for good or ill, or perhaps for both. Whether we like it or not, computers present us with new moral and, yes, spiritual choices, especially when they are connected together in cyberspace (which we'll explore more in Chapter 3). Ignoring these choices does not mean they will not get made: they will simply be made by others, or perhaps be made by default.

One trouble is that computers, information technology, the Internet, cyberspace and so on are surrounded by such a tremendous fog of technological jargon and mystique that ordinary people feel they are powerless to understand, let alone affect, what is going on. Three attitudes to computers and information technology are common.

- **The enthusiast**, who gives an uncritical welcome to everything hi-tech. Progress is good, experts are to be trusted and critics are Luddites. The trouble here is that the enthusiast risks being so dazzled by the benefits of technological progress that he or she neglects its less desirable consequences.

1

- **The ostrich.** Many people feel that they don't understand computers, and hence (often implicitly) can have no opinions about,
or influence on, their use in society. Our view is that information
technology is having such a pervasive and profound impact on
the society we live in that it is far too important to leave to the
'experts'; that is, to a combination of politicians and professionals, however well intentioned.

- **The prophet of doom,** whose main theme is a litany of stories
about the incompetence of, or harmful effects of, computer systems. Such blanket condemnation is ineffective; IT is not going to
be uninvented, nor would we argue that it should be. More
importantly, though, this view does not open us up to the creative potential that IT can unlock.

Our purpose is to encourage an informed awareness about these
changes, to encourage users of the technology to reflect on its meaning
for them, and to think about how it may serve their needs. Our aim is
not to evangelize on behalf of the technology, proclaiming what great
things computers are, and how much all our readers need one (if they
do not have one), or need a newer, smarter, more powerful one (if they
already have one). Plenty of people do that already! Nor is it to decry
the technology as such. There is no clear and simple answer to be given
to the question whether IT or the Internet are 'good things', though people may (and do) do good things with them. The overriding concern is
that we see the technologies discussed in the light of human good and
human flourishing.

So what's new?

Of course, any technological advance opens up new avenues. So what
is different about computers? We suggest several ways in which computers are distinctively different from most technological advances.

First, their use is pervasive. A new kind of life jacket is important for
sailors and canoeists, but it is not going to affect the lives of many of us
directly. In contrast, computers reach every corner of our lives. Cash
machines, anti-lock brakes, microwave ovens, toasters, watches, mobile
phones, video recorders, direct-line insurance, supermarket checkouts,
personal letter-writing . . . the list goes on.

Second, their impact is profound. There comes a point when technology makes a *qualitative* change to the way we live, rather than just a quantitative one. In particular, *computers affect our relationships with each other.* Electronic mail, ubiquitous mobile phones, video conferencing, Internet chat rooms, personal web sites, bulletin boards each give us a new way of relating to each other. These new forms of communication profoundly affect our social fabric. Geographically dispersed special interest groups can form, which would otherwise be impossible. Email is wonderful because it makes it possible to contact someone quickly but without requiring them to be available at the precise moment of the call . . . and terrible too because it is so easy to send 'spam' mail to hundreds of thousands of unwilling recipients.

Computers affect how we think of ourselves, and what we think of as real. Computers have always been engaging, even addictive, to some. As they become more sophisticated, that appeal becomes more widespread. A great deal of effort goes into creating 'virtual reality' worlds, sometimes for entertainment, sometimes for more prosaic purposes (such as letting an architect 'walk through' an unbuilt building). The outcome is to blur the boundary between us and the machine.

All of this raises interesting philosophical questions, but our interest here is more pragmatic: how do computers affect us, as individuals, and in our relationships with others, and in our relationship with God?

Computers are unusual in having both these qualities. Hamburgers, for example, are pervasive, but do not have a profound impact. Artificial hip replacement has a profound impact on the lives of those it affects directly, but is not pervasive. Computers are both. Not only that, but the best, or worst, is yet to come. So far the impact of computers has been more profound than pervasive. We do not yet have essentially free communication of really large quantities of information over very large distances. There is not yet a satellite dish in every Indian village. Truly immersive virtual reality systems are still expensive and cartoon-like. Information about us as individuals is still distributed among a thousand incompatible databases. But these things will change, and in ways that no one can accurately predict.

Beyond this, computers have a **third** extraordinary, even unique, characteristic: **they transcend familiar physical limits.** Much of the world we are used to is governed, in one way or another, by physical limits. Computers and digital communication networks do away with many such limits; in particular, *they make it possible to copy, manipulate and transmit digital information essentially for nothing.* This ability has complex and unpredictable consequences. For example:

- **Digitized information can be duplicated cheaply with no loss of quality,** whether it is a database, a computer program, a video, the design of an aeroplane, or the digital representation of a book or a work of art. All these things could be copied before, but there always used to be some significant physical cost associated with it, even if it was only standing in front of the photocopier for a few hours. Furthermore, the copy was usually less perfect than the original.

- **Digitized information can be encrypted cheaply and perfectly.** This makes it possible for people to have digital conversations that are almost impossible to tap, with benefits for privacy, and costs for law enforcement.

- **Digitized information can be transmitted from one place to another cheaply, and with no degradation.** This 'death of distance' makes new relationships and communities possible that would otherwise be impractical. It also makes possible hitherto physically unattainable concentrations of power, and the much-discussed globalization of markets and trade. The East India Company was an international company but, when communication with head office took two months, local discretion was unavoidable. Now, one head office, even one person, can take decisions that have immediate, global effects.

So far we have spoken simply of 'computers', which might be interpreted narrowly as meaning simply the raw 'hardware' (electronics) and 'software' (programs) of computer systems. But the whole point of this book is that the unique characteristics of computers that we have sketched above have given birth to something qualitatively new.

'Information technology' and 'the Internet' get closer to the 'something' that we have in mind, but they are still technologically oriented terms. The word we have chosen to focus on instead is 'cyberspace'. We will have more to say about what we mean by cyberspace in Chapter 2.

Good dreams, bad dreams

In what way are computers 'dream machines'? Dreams can express our aspirations, our hopes and longings. Dreams are also things that we never fully control. Computers belong to dream worlds in at least these two ways: they help us realize possibilities (fulfil our dreams), and they (like most technology) appear to develop a power all of their own, to become dreams we 'inhabit'.

We want to begin by affirming our excitement about the opportunities that computers can offer. Computers multiply human effort to a sometimes extraordinary degree. At their best, for example:

- **Their effective use creates wealth.** Computers now represent a major element of investment expenditure in many types of business. Their use helps us to increase both the quantity and quality of output, reduces repetitive tasks undertaken by employees and enhances access to information. Higher output can be achieved in this way. The overall effect is likely to be in enhanced economic growth with all the benefits that produces. However, not all members in society benefit equally in the first instance, since for some, job opportunities may be lost leading to the need for retraining and relocation. But a dynamic business environment will always give rise to such situations, which must be dealt with through social and employment policies.

- **They empower people and give them new levels of education.** Computers provide many excellent encyclopedias and electronic books. Unlike books, some of these are interactive and allow the reader to understand more about, say, environmental issues. Computers with networks give direct access to people and to knowledge, for example to library catalogues or museums, from around the world. You want to know how to help some cause or run a pressure group or a support group? It's all there, and you can participate and contribute. Access to information is subversive of totalitarian establishments of all kinds. There is a proud tradition of public libraries that the Internet is, in a more anarchic way, continuing.

- **They automate routine tasks.** They allow us to edit drafts of a document (such as this one) without continually retyping it; they remove the labour of searching thick files for elusive records;

they turn tables of figures into charts and graphs; they digest huge quantities of scientific data into a manageable pile of information; they do not get tired of monitoring safety conditions on a railway.

- **They support a flexible response to individual needs.** It can be a wonderful thing to talk to a customer support person who has immediate access to one's records.

- **They empower individuals.** Through the Internet, an individual has access to a truly vast library of information.

- **They support new forms of work and communication.** Traditional 9-to-5 work patterns suit many, but not all. IT enables people to work from home, and to collaborate with others who are far away, and possibly even in different time zones.

- **They are fun!** Computer-programming is fun. Computer games are fun. Virtual reality is fun. We do not mean to trivialize matters here. Human beings are built with a huge, God-given capacity for enjoyment, and it seems clear that computers offer a rich new environment for that enjoyment.

Each item in this list needs a caveat: some dreams are nightmares. Wealth is not something to be sought for its own sake. No word processor can turn drivel into pearls of wisdom. An insurance agent whose computer goes down may be utterly helpless. The Internet has much junk as well as much joy. Telecommuting is lonely. Computer games can be addictive. And so on.

Indeed, some of the 'good' things in the list above are 'good' largely because of other changes which have made them seem necessary, have *made* them good. Once upon a time, the insurance agent would have known all the customers on the firm's books, and dealt with them personally. Moving to systems with less personal contact, where the relationship is directly with a firm rather than the person, may be cheaper, and that is a benefit, but it is not a benefit without a cost.

All technologies have at once extended and limited people. Books, for example, encourage sharing ideas, and they also provide a substitute for human memory. Who needs to memorize a song if it is in the songbook? Books have helped to change our culture from one where older people were esteemed for their knowledge of tradition and folk memory to one where these skills are no longer so valued. It is probably too early to say what cyberspace will displace, and indeed whether we might regret its passing. It's not clear, either, whether the loss of memory skills is such a bad cost to pay for the vast benefits of books. However, stories from books – verses from the Bible – can fill the minds of people when they can no longer read, and give them sustenance in a society that may give them little else, and we have lost that.

In short, one of the most daunting things about computers is that they are so terribly good and so terribly bad at the same time. Neutral they are not.

Choosing our dreams

Technology is a means to fulfil our dreams, but how do we select which dreams? The question of whether a technology will actually work (whether it will do what we want it to) is, after all, distinct from whether the end is good. We need to reflect upon this basic question, because it runs to the heart of some of the most difficult debates we are facing. More precisely, *we believe that computers present us with a whole raft of moral dilemmas, some old ones in new guises and some new ones.* These dilemmas arise for several reasons:

1.   **Old questions appear in a new light**, and our existing intellectual and legal frameworks for presenting the issues do not scale to the new situation. We can see that there are questions about how things ought to be done, and that the answers to those questions matter. However, our tools for handling these questions seem to lack purchase on the material we are dealing with; they were designed for other contexts. To take just one example, national laws don't work well in cyberspace, which knows no borders.

2.   **New dilemmas arise from the new technological possibilities that computers offer.** If the transmission of data is absolutely safe and secure, beyond any possibility of interception, all sorts of dangerous possibilities may be opened up. How should we handle them? Should we restrict the availability of the encryption technology? (See Chapter 6.)

3.   **We have to grapple with whole new moral dimensions.** While we can describe the new situations and possibilities we are presented with, we are not yet able to evaluate them.

4. **It's all happening so fast.** It takes a while to digest, debate, and form opinions about a new moral question, and time to learn from experience. Yet it seems that we hardly have time to appreciate the complexities of one, still less agree about what to do about it, before the next one is upon us.

Over the centuries we have evolved in Britain a sort of moral consensus about right and wrong. This broad consensus is embodied in our laws and embedded in our cultural assumptions. This consensus is not explicitly based on a Christian understanding, but it has evolved from one that certainly was. While a Christian might find certain aspects that he or she would like to change, the broad setting is largely in tune with Christianity: respect for persons, property and freedom, and condemnation of violence, discrimination and exploitation, and so on.

As time goes on, this shared moral consensus shifts, fragments and reforms. Sometimes such adjustments are a response to changing attitudes (for example, towards gender), and sometimes they are in response to new situations (such as the industrial revolution, or immigration). However it happens, though, the process is usually rather gradual. We have developed a host of effective, albeit fallible, ways to debate and evolve such changes: through newspapers, magazines, books, elections, common law, and so on.

The interesting thing about computers is that *they force us to re-evaluate significant areas of our shared moral consensus.* Not only that, but they force us to do so so much faster than usual that our established mechanisms for evolving a new consensus are left far behind. Here are several examples:

• **Computers store and share personal information.** The law restricts access to computer-based medical and criminal information about individuals as it does with paper-based records. However, all other sorts of information, which was difficult to collate in a paper-based world, can now be efficiently gathered, assimilated and shared by computers. The Data Protection Act 1984 requires those with whom electronically stored data are to be shared to be registered at the time of entering the data. Companies, by dint of broad-brush registering, can accrue the right to pass on details they may hold about individuals. Hence an individual, once having given information about him- or herself to a company, for example through a customer satisfaction questionnaire, has released these details into cyberspace. They can then be made available, easily, to those who request it. Information of different sorts given to different companies can be correlated by means of identifiers such as postcode and surname. Personal profiles, created, added to and passed around in this way, erode our sense of privacy, independence and, above all, freedom.

- **Computers can duplicate information at essentially no cost.** In the physical world, it is not easy to replicate an object, but in cyberspace thousands of copies of data can be made on your home PC in seconds. This dramatic reduction in the cost of copying is placing immense strain on the legal framework of copyright. The point is not that we simply need to invent new laws. Rather, we first need to work out what is right and wrong in this new arena. (For example, many people who would think it hugely wrong to steal a bicycle from a shop do not find it wrong to take a copy of a software program that would be sold for hundreds of pounds.) Somehow the fact that the copy does not appear to cost the original owner anything, nor to deprive the owner of anything, shifts many people's moral balance.

- **Computers offer new forms of 'free speech'.** Our culture values freedom of speech very highly, and in many ways the Internet makes free speech freer. It is easier both to publish and to find information than hitherto. But not all speech is good. We accept a number of specific limitations to free speech, such as slander, libel, incitement to racial hatred, pornography and so on. The laws against such things are always controversial, but they don't affect many of us. The nature of physical media makes it possible to control access to offensive material; pornographic magazines must be placed on a high shelf. Such control is much more difficult in cyberspace. International boundaries are crossed, offensive material might be encrypted so that it is not easily recognizable, and so on. The Internet forces us to reopen the moral question of what should and should not be said in public.

- **Computers are opaque and unpredictable.** Much conventional technology (from bicycles to washing machines) is transparent and predictable: we can see how it works, predict what it will do and what it won't do, and have a go at fixing it if it breaks. Even something as complicated as an aeroplane is fairly predictable: if you put more cargo into it, it may fly a bit less well, and eventually it won't get off the ground; but it is most unlikely that the wings will suddenly fall off when you add a single matchstick.

Computers are quite different. A computer is a completely opaque black box. Its workings are silent, hidden and, most of the time, flawless. For this reason, computers often inspire a sort of uncritical trust. But this trust is often misplaced: computers fail horribly, and (worse) entirely unpredictably, when they encounter a situation that their designers did not anticipate – the year 2000 problem is a notorious example. Very small changes in input, or very rare events, can cause complete and catastrophic failure.

One could argue that this raises practical, rather than moral, questions. Is it a moral question if my car refuses to start because of a bug in its software? The wider dimension is this: the more pervasive computers are, the more trust we are forced to place in the perfection of the engineers that built them, and the less ability we have to respond flexibly to technological failure. How far do we want to move in that direction?

- **Computers may become so integral to our lives and bodies that we literally cannot live without them.** Nowadays you can carry a 'smart' identity card in your pocket, that opens the security doors of an office building. It is only a short step for that card to be implanted in your arm – so convenient, it never gets lost. Within the lifetime of many of us, computers will help blind people to see and deaf people to hear, by linking directly into their nervous systems. All of this is awesome, but troubling. Will the blind be seeing what is really there, or something else?

In each case, the pervasive influence of computers forces us to address moral questions. But since these questions fall outside the territory of our shared consensus we have to figure out right and wrong all over again. That in turn requires us to have a moral framework, and that is where Christians have something to offer.

What this book is for

As authors of this book we came to some clear conclusions about the significance of computer technology during our meetings to discuss the text. These have been briefly laid out in this chapter. To summarize:

1. The impact of computers is both pervasive and profound.

2. The effect of computers on us as individuals and on society is not neutral: they present us with both enormous benefits and enormous problems at the same time.

3. This forces us to address moral questions which fall outside the territory of our shared moral consensus, so we have to figure out right and wrong all over again.

It is the purpose of this book to provide the reader with some tools with which to tackle the moral and spiritual questions raised by computer use. Since the book was written by a group of Christians it is to that tradition we have naturally turned. It has been our experience in the rest of our lives that insights from the Bible and other parts of the Christian tradition can give us both a moral framework and the sense of identity that are necessary to equip us to deal with new moral challenges as they arise. It is our belief and hope that non-Christians will also have much to gain from this approach.

2
What is Cyberspace?

In this chapter we explain some of the basic concepts of cyberspace. In looking at the technology we can begin to see that it is not something separate from the rest of our lives, but is already intrinsically woven into the fabric of our society: the ways we live and the way we think. Digital communications have thrown open new worlds of experience, virtual worlds in which we are dealing with new forms of reality. Digital information has characteristics which change the way we think, for instance, our sense of space – geographical location is no longer important – and our notions of truth. We conclude that the sheer scale of cyberspace, its impact and growth, present us with challenges which we need to understand in order to tackle them.

Cyberspace! The word was coined by William Gibson, in a classic (albeit rather depressing) science fiction novel, *Neuromancer* (1984). We take 'cyberspace' as our principal theme, rather than 'computers' or 'information technology' or 'the Internet', partly because it is so evocative. It suggests that the computer world now supports a new and real social 'space' – one that raises more questions about people than about technology.

So, what does cyberspace mean to us? Cyberspace is worldwide and respects no nation's frontiers: it reaches from the recesses of Mongolia to the many-varied cultures of California; it includes Benedictine monks and the Mullahs in Iraq; it gives people everywhere access to digitized images of the rare treasures in the Louvre and the British Library; it gives people in inner London guided tours of dinosaur museums in Canada. Our children are using it to do their school projects on the lives of sperm whales off the coast of New Zealand. We can see the latest Hubble telescope pictures of space.

In short, much of human life is represented in cyberspace. On a personal level the impact is profound. People meet in cyberspace, work in it, play in it, learn things and discover things in it. Increasingly, people's relationships, jobs and money will take place in cyberspace, and that makes it important.

The impact on society is perhaps already larger than many have had opportunity to appreciate. Here is a simple example. London tea trading started 300 years ago, and the auction rooms were a place where people could come together. Now, the Internet has enabled producers in countries like Kenya and Sri Lanka to set up their own auctions, without involving London. One community has been destroyed, and power has shifted, in this case, from the London centre to the producing countries themselves.

Cyberspace is far from the first example of the way in which a technological change can have profound personal and social impact. To give an historical example, railways were seen as 'just machinery' until people realized that you no longer needed lots of local factories; instead you could have one centralized factory, and transport the goods it made by rail. That in turn led to more railways, and greater opportunity to centralize the production of goods, and to decide where they were located. The railway system was more than the mechanics of the railway, and more than the mechanisms of running a railway. It transformed the notion of distance. Cyberspace is having a similar transforming effect, and it is happening right before our eyes.

The really important issues, then, are to do with people. But to grapple with them we first need to describe the bricks and mortar that support cyberspace and its developments. This chapter explores what cyberspace is, and some of the ways in which it changes our thinking.

Digital communications

The main characteristic of cyberspace is that it involves communication, in many new forms. Asking what sort of communication happens in cyberspace is rather like asking what a road is. The word 'road' covers mountain tracks to motorways, and the so-called 'information superhighway' has many facets, too. The essential thing to grasp is not whether something is a mountain track, road or railway, but the general concept of each being part of a travel and transport system.

The Internet

This is the worldwide network of 'telephone wires' that enable one person to access or receive digital information from another. The wires (and radio links and other sorts of links) make networks that connect computers together. The Internet is the network of networks. Everything on it agrees on a basic protocol (rather as car drivers agree to drive on the same side of the road). The point of the protocol is that all the computers can communicate with each other, and in the best case things shouldn't get lost.

The Internet is growing extraordinarily fast. Between 1970 and 1981 computer networks grew 'modestly' at 20–30 per cent per year. Then all these separate networks were connected to form an 'inter-network', and the Internet was born. Since 1983 the Internet has, on average, more than doubled in size every year. Anything that doubles every year gets very, very large: in 1981 around 200 computers were attached to a typical big network; at the end of 1998, more than 20,000,000 were connected to the Internet.

Internet Service Providers

Internet Service Providers (ISPs) are the companies that connect you to the Internet. Your computer makes a dial-up connection to the ISP, using an ordinary telephone line. The ISP has a direct connection to the Internet itself, and it makes the link between your dial-up connection and the net (via a computer, of course). There are many ISPs in Britain, and they advertise in the daily papers.

Electronic mail

Electronic mail (email) is the computer version of mail. Just as anyone with a road might get postal mail, anyone connected to the Internet can get email. There are several subtle differences about email: because computers are involved, the relation between senders and recipients is changed. For example, it is possible to send anonymous email easily; whether this technical facility is used for whistle-blowing, secret ballots, unanswerable libel or blackmail depends on how people choose to use it.

An important characteristic of email is that – once you get used to it – it feels as easy to use as a telephone, but it does not rely on the other person's being there just at the right time. Nor is it real-time: as with letter-writing, but contrary to the case with a phone call, we can pause to think what to say. Indeed, the fact that we 'put things into' cyberspace, and later on we or someone else 'take things out', is part of why we think of cyberspace as a 'space' at all. It contains things, which is what places or spaces do.

Like a letter, an email is a one-way communication. We do not get the nods and grunts that give us feedback in our spoken communication. People tend to think carefully about what they write in a letter, but the immediacy of email makes it surprisingly easy to dash off a message that causes unintentional offence. Experienced cybernauts write their messages with care.

Amnesty International has found email of invaluable assistance in communicating without having all its mail monitored, particularly in the early days of the Internet. Now it is used to send many messages to relevant government departments about injustices. Email is effective for these purposes because it is easy to use and so many people use it to draw attention to injustices – and politicians take note of the numbers of messages they receive.

Bulletin boards

Bulletin boards (BBSs) are the cyberspace equivalent of noticeboards. People can post notices and reply to notices, either using the bulletin board or by using email. Because the Internet is so large, it supports thousands of bulletin boards. Almost every human interest is covered by bulletin boards – and if your particular interest isn't there, it is quite easy to create a new one. One possible use of a bulletin board is to share experience between people suffering from rare medical disorders; in this way, you may find the other three people in the world with the same condition and exchange advice. Another use of a bulletin board is to be a collection point for information, say for some environmental cause. In contrast to the World Wide Web, which is more like a giant magazine, bulletin boards are sustained by the conversations of the people using them.

The World Wide Web

The World Wide Web made the Internet truly popular, because it made it very easy for the Internet to embrace pictures and sound. Although originally invented to help scientists, the web enabled the Internet to support entertainment and advertising on a huge, popular scale. The web is rather like a worldwide magazine, where anyone can contribute pages. There are pages 'written' on behalf of Swedish hamsters, and there are pages written by governments. There are pages with live TV images of volcanoes, and there are pages with ancient documents from the world's great museums.

Much of this information is provided by governments, universities or companies. But much is also provided by individuals: the web makes it extremely easy to publish material yourself, from photos of your new baby to instructions on how to build a Roman catapult or a home-made bomb. Historically, it has been the big players that have originated, or at least mediated, most publications. They have been the producers and we have been the consumers. We can all be worldwide producers now, and that is something new.

Browsers

Of all of the ways of accessing cyberspace, browsers are (at least at the moment) the most visible. A browser is the program that runs on your computer, and allows you access to the web. It lets you read web pages and follow links they contain, sends and receives email, reads and contributes to bulletin boards, and so on. It is, figuratively, your window on the web. Indeed, people may use their computer for nothing else but running a browser.

Search engines

These are programs that make a sort of index of web pages. The best known build this index by reading all the web pages they can find, and extracting key words or phrases from them. They have to run on very large servers (computers permanently attached to the Internet which provide services to other computers) because the web is enormous, so even an index of the web is very large indeed. You talk to a search engine using (naturally) your browser. You type the words you want to find, say 'Swedish hamster', into a little box, and press a button; your words are sent to the server, which looks them up in its index, and turns the results into a new web page, especially for you; this new web page is sent back to your computer and displayed by your browser.

By using search engines, the cyberspace version of telephone directories, we can find web pages based on what they contain, and not only by their cyberspace 'addresses'. If you want to find a Swedish hamster, you don't need to know it by name – as you would if you used a telephone directory service. You can find it by its description. Interestingly, search engines are one of the rapidly changing areas of cyberspace: they are too good for their own good! A search for hamsters will find you more hamsters than you could possibly cope with.

Virtual worlds

So cyberspace lets us communicate and share information with each other. If that were all, we would hardly call it a space. But, cyberspace is a two-way thing: like the real world, we are affected by cyberspace and affect it. It contains 'virtual worlds'. For example, the Internet can be used for showing TV pictures – a one-way process. Just as we might imagine ourselves into a TV film, we can imagine ourselves into a cyberspace 'film'. But more, we can interact with other people also imagining themselves into the story, and now the process becomes two-way. We begin to get a sense of a 'virtual world'. There are a huge range of virtual worlds in cyberspace: some are realistic three-dimensional worlds, and others are rather more like the imaginary worlds we create in our heads when we read a novel – based almost entirely on text. Some virtual worlds are games, and they can be very addictive games, often involving role-playing where the players are fantasy heroes (generally with magical and spiritual overtones). Some virtual worlds are quite literally serious business, as when a worldwide company wants to run a high-level conference.

Internet Relay Chat

Internet Relay Chat (IRC) is a very popular form of virtual world. It is quite cheap and accessible – it only uses text, and therefore relies more on people's imagination. So, IRC is more like a conference telephone call than a shared TV experience. With IRC, chat rooms are created where people can drop in and discuss whatever they like. Sometimes, some of the participants in chat rooms will actually be computers, with their own characters. Some chat rooms are used for role-playing games (like the fantasy game Dungeons and Dragons); these are often called MUDs, or Multi-User Dungeons.

Total-immersion virtual reality

From the human perspective, a virtual world becomes virtual reality when we cannot tell or are no longer concerned about the difference between it and reality. Long ago, when a lion jumped out at you, you wouldn't stop and think whether it was a picture or not – you'd run, or pray, or probably both! If something looked like a lion, it was a lion, and your survival would have depended on your never pausing to worry about the difference. Now images in virtual reality hit our senses as if they were real. Provided we don't look beyond the edge of the screen, the images landing on our retinas are very close to real images. In other words, virtual reality is real as far as our emotional reactions and our instant responses are concerned.

The power of this virtual reality is enormous. People can be trained to fly aircraft without any of the physical dangers of flying (or firing missiles at the wrong targets); and at the other end of the spectrum, cyberspace can create sexual fantasies that are 'real' without any of the responsibilities required in reality. There are commercial products to support each of these applications. Many fear that people will immerse themselves in false models of the world, intentionally or otherwise, when what is needed is action in society and the environment to sustain life.

On being digital

The defining characteristic of the technology (computers, networks, storage devices, and so on) that supports cyberspace is that it is *digital*. Traditionally, information has been stored in *analogue* form, as (say) the shape of ink marks on a page, the strength of a magnetic field on an audio tape, or the depth of a groove on a vinyl record.

Information stored *digitally* is stored simply as a *sequence of numerical values*. These numerical values are represented in the binary number system in computers, as binary digits, known as *bits*. It is initially surprising that virtually any information can be (and is) stored and transmitted digitally:

- **Text**, such as the contents of this book, or an electronic mail message, is easy to store digitally; just imagine assigning a number to each letter of the alphabet. Adding some extra information to describe the formatting of the text is not much harder.

- **Sounds.** We have all become familiar with audio CDs, which store music digitally. Telephone conversations usually work over analogue wires as far as the local telephone exchange, but after that they are converted to digital form and routed over the trunk network.

  How can sounds be reduced to a sequence of numerical values? Simply by measuring the height of the sound waveform at regular intervals, and using that as the sequence. To play back the sound, feed the numbers to an electronic gadget (a digital-to-analogue converter in the jargon) that outputs an electronic signal whose size is controlled by the sequence of numbers, and connect the output to a loudspeaker. In the timescales of computers, sound waves are fairly slow: we can only hear sounds that vibrate up to about 20,000 times a second, which gives plenty of time for a computer to do the sampling and recording. (A computer's heart, or 'clock', beats around 400,000,000 times a second in 1998.)

- **Pictures** can be expressed in digital form too. First, divide the picture up into very small squares, called *pixels*. Now, express how much red, how much green, and how much blue colour there is in that pixel, as three numerical values. Give these three numbers for each pixel, and you have described a complete picture.

  Reverse the same process to display a digital picture. Computer screens (like televisions) display colours by having lots of tiny red, blue and green dots next to each other; by lighting them up with brightness controlled by those numbers, we can make the original picture appear on the screen.

  Digital television has just had its debut in Britain, and digital cameras are becoming more widespread; both work in this way. Pictures are much greedier than sounds. Even one colour picture on a 500 x 500 pixel grid takes 750,000 numbers to express fully, and a full video requires many pictures each second. So, in the digital world, a picture costs much more than a thousand words; a word takes only a handful of numbers! That is why your web browser often goes very slowly when it is receiving pictures over the Internet. Clever compression techniques, which can be applied to any digital data, can, however, reduce the amount of data that must be stored or transmitted. These techniques are particularly effective on pictures which have a lot of redundancy (e.g. large areas of a single colour).

- **Personal information** based on an individual's actions ranges from recording purchases made in shops, preferred spending patterns (from bank accounts), movements caught on CCTV or inferred from mobile phone movements or car navigation systems, through to the choices made when viewing web pages.

- **Money** has always been somewhat virtual, because banks have always lent much more money than they actually have in their vaults. Nowadays, people, businesses and banks send each other money electronically. Of course, there is more involved than just sending the amount! Somehow it has to be impossible (or at least very difficult) to forge such electronic cash.

In short, *anything that can be measured can be represented digitally*. For example, computers can record the contours of someone's face or heart, so that surgeons can show it on the screen from any angle and practise complicated surgery on your simulated body. Computers can record details of someone's body movements, so those movements can be used to train someone else, or to tell a computer how to make a computer-animated image move realistically (this was done in some of the long-distance shots in the film *Titanic*). But there are some things that can't easily be represented in digital form, like love, and terror.

This apparently simple ability to represent virtually anything digitally has huge implications. In the analogue world, the storage and transmission methods for different kinds of information were quite different. Pictures were on paper, sounds were stored on cassette tape or vinyl records, video was stored on VHS cassettes, and so on. The cable television network was separate from the telephone network, which was separate from the (now outdated) telex network. In the digital world, all that changes. The same CD can store a song, a picture or a document, because they are all represented as bits. The same network can transmit any of these things. This is provoking a huge upheaval in the telephone and television industries, as their businesses blur into the computer network industry.

Beyond physical limits

Beyond all this, changing from analogue to digital form gives cyberspace an extraordinary, even unique, characteristic: **it transcends familiar physical limits**, and this lack of familiar physical limits lies at the heart of the perplexing opportunities of cyberspace.

Much of the world we are used to is governed, in one way or another, by physical limits. Cars, no matter how expensive, can only go so fast. People, no matter how talented, can only work for 24 hours in a day (at most). Computers and digital communication networks do away with many such limits; in particular, they make it possible to copy, manipulate and transmit digital information essentially for nothing. This ability has complex and unpredictable consequences. Here are some examples.

Digital information does not degrade

An audio cassette tape wears out; and if it is re-recorded on to a new tape, the new recording is never quite the same as the original. In the same way, a photocopy is not *exactly* the same as the original.

In contrast, digital information can be reproduced perfectly, time after time. There is no mystery to this: if you were given a list of numbers, even written in bad handwriting, you could transcribe them accurately, and someone else could copy your work, and so on for ever. The recording has been, up to a point, set free from the medium on which it is stored.

Even if some numbers do get lost in transit (perhaps the bad handwriting became illegible in one or two places) there are ways to correct for that. For example, you could store everything twice, and reckon that the chances of an error happening twice in the same place would be low. Delightfully cunning ways have been developed to correct errors in digital documents with much less overhead than storing them twice. Your mobile phone is doing this every time you use it.

There is an irony here, because while digital information can indeed be reproduced perfectly, the physical devices on which it is usually stored are much less robust than the traditional analogue storage mechanism, writing on paper or papyrus. We can still read documents written hundreds, or sometimes thousands, of years ago. But a floppy disk deteriorates in a few years, and even if kept carefully there might be no floppy disk drives available in a hundred years, let alone a thousand. The more sophisticated the medium (hard disk, CD) the more sophisticated the device needed to read it, and the less likely such devices are to be available in a hundred years. Instead, better, faster, smaller devices will be in use; but that doesn't help with a hundred-year-old CD, even if the CD has not deteriorated physically, which no one knows for sure.

So digital information is simultaneously more robust and more fragile than analogue information.

Digital information can be manipulated more readily

A physical document can be photocopied in its exact form, and sent to others. In contrast an electronic document can be edited, reordered, reformatted (for example, changing the page layout or font), checked for errors of spelling or grammar, indexed, sent to others by email, published on the web, and so on. All of this is much easier because the information is stored digitally.

All sorts of digital information can be manipulated, not just text. Altering a physical photograph is difficult, and relatively easy to detect. Altering an electronic photograph, though, is just a matter of changing some of the numbers. Manipulation is so easy that it is hard to know what is visual truth. Another example is the way in which someone can sing into a microphone, a computer analyses the recorded sound, deduce that it is out of tune and then correct it before putting it out over the speakers. Indeed, one can already go further and have the singer's voice sound like someone famous, the voice transformed into the characteristic vocal harmonic spectrum of that famous person.

Digital information can be transmitted efficiently

Information in analogue form more or less has to be transmitted all at once. But the Internet transmits digital information in small chunks called *packets*. Your email message (or whatever) is chopped into packets and fed into the Internet; sooner or later most of them will arrive at the destination; the destination will ask the sender to retransmit any packets that got lost; and finally it will reconstruct your original message. Nowadays, this happens for your phone conversations too!

All of this is very different from the analogue way of working. The old phone networks would dedicate a particular piece of wire to a single conversation, even during the parts of your conversation when neither of you were saying anything. The ability to chop everything into packets and then just process the packets individually in any order makes it possible to carry huge numbers of different messages, conversations, stock trades, web accesses, or whatever, on a single wire

It turns out that the cost of transmitting a packet from A to B no longer depends much on where A and B are. That is, in reality it is just about as cheap to send a packet from London to Hong Kong as from London to Hatfield. This 'death of distance' has yet to manifest itself in local rate phone calls direct to Hong Kong, but that is now due more to commercial and political factors than technical ones.

Digitization changes geography

One of the litmus tests of whether something is in cyberspace is whether its location counts. If you were to ask, for example, 'Where is this digital object that I am using?', the answer would often come 'I don't know and it doesn't matter.' In using the web, you look at a page of information delivered to your computer from the USA, click on a link that implies the next information page comes from a non-profit company in India, then another that is in Australia and then . . . After a few steps the location ceases to matter. Information is digitized but its geographical physical location is not important. Even if one knew, the location could be changed very rapidly to another digital 'space' on earth, or even stored in a memory on a satellite. Just as the music recording was set free from the medium in which it was stored, so the digital object is set free from location. There must be some storage medium; the data must be somewhere. But what and where generally don't matter.

Digital documents can be put in practically unbreakable code

Cryptography concerns the 'coding' of data, so that it cannot be read by unauthorized people. Codes have been around for millennia, but computers have driven recent (post -1950) developments in so-called strong cryptographic techniques. These techniques make it possible to take any digital information (picture, sound, money, it doesn't make any difference) and encode it in such a way that no one who does not have the key to the code can understand it.

Strong code techniques raise important questions about privacy and security; they will have a role in cyberspace, but what that role should be is still under debate.

Digitization affects what we think of as a 'thing'

We are used to thinking of money, for example, as having some physical form that is very difficult to copy; now money takes electronic form and banks take enormous care not to duplicate it by accident. We are used to thinking of a book as something with physical form, consisting of a certain number of original, identical copies; now, an electronic document may be altered on a daily basis by its author, and may be read or copied at any moment.

Even the physical limits that computers do have are being driven back at an astonishing pace. In 1980 a personal computer with 64,000 bytes of memory was considered vastly luxurious. Now it is common to find personal computers with 60,000,000 bytes of memory. A now rather hackneyed, but still useful, analogy is this: imagine if, over the same period, your car went 1,000 times as far on a gallon of petrol, or your house was 1,000 times as big for the same money.

In practice, the principal limitation on the scale and sophistication of computer systems is no longer their speed or memory capacity, but our own inability to imagine, design, and build the software that animates them. The complexity of these software monsters is daunting, and tales of commercial software disasters are commonplace. We cannot blame the medium, as a carpenter or a bridge designer can. Instead, we are face to face with our own intellectual shortcomings – not a bad thing, perhaps.

Cyberspace: what lies ahead?

It is tempting to see cyberspace as having emerged from nowhere over the last 40 years. In fact, however, human beings have been engaged in transcending the 'here and now' of their physical bodies for a long time – seeking to leave messages for others, record events in stone and on papyri and, earlier, in oral traditions. These examples illustrate that many people are involved in the process of transcending the 'here and now' – reed-cutters and collectors, papyri-makers, writers, alphabet-developers, thinkers, organizers, archivists – in fact a whole system comprising people and mechanisms. Their basic characteristic is to move some action or aspect of life from particular individuals and specific machines to a more generalized and impersonal system so that it can be picked up and used by different people and devices at a variety of times and places. Papyri and books meant that people could read what had previously only been passed down in stories, person to person. Recordings of music mean that people can hear concerts performed far away and generations earlier.

Cyberspace is following a similar development in the much broader category of information and knowledge, and moving the knowledge and skills that were only held in people's bodies towards a new system. These times have often been called the 'Information Age' because information and knowledge are made available and usable at a distance from the individual or organization who knew it, created it, or acted it.

So cyberspace is not wholly a new phenomenon. But computers are unlike anything we have ever had, because they can do creative things on their own even when there is no one around to supervise them. A bank might have used telephones to provide phone banking, but cash machines can provide many features of banking without any bank cashiers being involved, and they can run at night. Cyberspace allows businesses to decentralize, perhaps even on an international scale, and yet not lose any control over their diffuse operations. As well as these new ideas, the scale of cyberspace, its pace of growth and its profound effects do present us with challenges, both personal and social, that we have not yet developed the means to handle. Cyberspace seems to have a momentum of its own; it develops without any central control, and new ramifications appear every day. The development of electrical power followed a similar course. First there was small-scale specialized use; then there was a period of explosive growth, enabled by the introduction of local electrical grids; after that point, the growth of new electrical goods, and the growth of the National Grid that powered them, fed off each other; and now it is hard to think of modern life without electricity.

We are now in the explosive-growth phase of cyberspace technology. It will happen with us or without us. Much of the specific content of this chapter will be dated in a few years, or even by the time it is published, but the underlying trend is already clear: cyberspace will become an ever more complex social space, in which more and more people will conduct more and more of their lives. The question is: what kind of cyberspace do we want?

3

Into Cyberspace

In this chapter we look in detail at some ways in which cyberspace is changing our thoughts, feelings and actions. Cyberspace is changing how we perceive truth: web sites may give the facts behind the stories but can mislead and misrepresent; it is changing the way we treat people: we can keep in touch and make friends by email but there is a risk of confusing the cyber-presence with the person; it is shifting power: anyone with a web site can reach the world but a few organizations have immense power; its diversity and complexity can be exhilarating but can cause alienation. And it is also challenging our understanding of what a person is. Computer programs can increasingly behave in cyberspace as if they were persons, challenging what it means to be human.

Technology changes what is possible. It also changes what we think of as possible. Ships, railways, motorcars and air travel changed the sense of geography and personal space. Printing, and postal, telegraph and telephone systems changed the means of sending messages and communication. There have been enormous changes in what we think is possible from the recent developments in travel, human reproduction and communication. Technology does more than just mechanically change possibilities, it changes what we think it is possible to accomplish.

So does cyberspace. New possibilities and habits are introduced by the power of rapid communication and access to information. The Internet alters the sense of space and time in what we can do and with whom we communicate. Because cyberspace is causing profound and pervasive changes, our minds are shaped by its changes, which are then reinforced by daily use and experience. It is what we do as well as what we think that shapes our minds; what we do regularly leads us into new habits. We stop thinking about what we do habitually. We come to expect the new capability.

Our expectation comes with a cost. The ability to manipulate digital objects makes us wonder if what we are looking at or hearing is real and true. Easy communication all over the globe makes us re-evaluate relationships as we spend time with people online. Or not. Most of us just survive and do not think about such questions – we simply accept the way that cyberspace and its new economy shapes our thoughts without thinking about it.

This chapter examines a few of the ways in which cyberspace is shaping our thinking, which we now consider here under the headings:

- What is true?
- What are real relationships?
- Who has the power?
- What is a person?

What is true?

Cyberspace raises the question 'What is true?' in lots of different guises. Here we focus on two. First, cyberspace can mislead us into a limited view of reality, something we call 'the stage effect'. Secondly, cyberspace makes possible new sorts of misrepresentation and impersonation, so things presented as real are not real.

The stage effect

When we watch a play, whether *Hamlet* or *Star Trek*, we become immersed in the drama. As it feels real, we suspend disbelief, and to the extent we do this we enjoy or become more deeply engaged in the drama. It becomes quite difficult to ask and think about questions, say, about the actors themselves, or about what goes on beyond the edge of the stage, or beyond the edge of the screen. For beyond the edge of the stage, the play does not exist – yet for our imaginations to work the play is real, and we forget it is only a view into a world, the whole of which does not exist. If it did exist, we could ask real questions, like 'Where are Captain Kirk's descendants today?' The stage effect suggests that something that is not complete can seem to be complete, so that we become largely unaware of its edges and limitations.

Cyberspace can very easily fill a person's whole awareness, and if you are not there, it is hard to be considered by those involved. Nearly all the authors of this report exchanged files by email – any who were not on email had difficulty keeping up with the rapidly unfolding drama of debate, edits and decisions. Academics searching computer library catalogues often find fewer than 40 per cent of the relevant articles, yet are unaware of missing the rest of the world. Many students do not investigate paper catalogues, preferring the online versions, and think that anything done 10 years ago must be superseded. As we look into cyberspace, we can get caught up in the drama of everything that is happening there and we can ignore the fact that the stage is limited. It is hard to remember that some are excluded from cyberspace – cyberspace seems so overwhelming as it is. In cyberspace, we simply don't see them in the first place.

Thus cyberspace can seem more complete than it is. One result is that people 'in' cyberspace and deeply experienced with it tend to overrate it. Their success in it requires a practised competence; at the same time, the people outside cyberspace are like the people who do not understand why *Star Trek* (or even Shakespeare) is worth watching and suspending disbelief for! The overrating by users and underappreciation by non-users leads to polarization and difficult entrenched debate.

Interestingly, this same stage effect can be seen in scientific research using computers to analyse data automatically. The computers recording measurements of the thickness of the ozone layer over the Antarctic were systematically throwing away data that indicated a growing hole. Why? Because all the scientists had assumed that the ozone layer would thin evenly and the computer had been programmed to identify any strange measurements as errors and throw them away. The computer programmers had got caught looking only at one 'stage'.

Distrust

Once we understand how easy it is to manipulate a digital object, we begin to distrust what we see. For example, if we know that any photograph, TV sequence or other recording could have been manipulated, this can lead to distrust. Similarly, because computer programs can be written to change certain words routinely (on the basis of some rule), people may be unsure whether the email they receive is the same as that which the sender wrote. Such concerns are the basis of much new cryptography, so that people can be (more) certain that what was sent is what was received.

Another source of distrust is the way that individuals can disguise who they really are through the Internet. For anyone who wants to be devious, the flexibility cyberspace provides is seductive. An adult might pretend to be a child, and use this role to gain the (misplaced) confidence of a real child. A person may pretend to want to enter into a sexual relationship with someone else, but mislead them as to their own sex. These possibilities can lead to something extraordinarily hurtful and damaging.

For some people, however, role-playing is entirely straightforward, and perhaps helps them free themselves of inhibitions or provides a lifeline release from prejudice. People sometimes shunned in real life can interact on equal terms with everyone else in cyberspace; using email, nobody need ever be aware that you can only walk, talk or write excruciatingly slowly, for instance.

Where deliberate concealment is practised or contemplated, we need to ask what the motive for it might be. The motive may be, amongst others, playful or educational, helpful or dishonest. The possibility of dishonest and maliciously deceptive uses of concealment cannot be ignored, though the anonymity of cyberspace may be the only condition under which some people may find the courage to seek counselling or to find help, so we cannot automatically assume the possibility of concealment to be a negative thing; in the practical context of daily living it may have its limited but positive uses.

What are real relationships?

New communication systems always raise questions about relationships. Will the nature of our relationships change? We suggest that use of cyberspace raises two different kinds of question: one about relationships, discussed more fully in Chapter 5, and another about our view of people, discussed here.

Neighbours and neo-tribes

In 'the old days' a tribe was a geographically gathered group of people. The word often has overtones of ignorance, because most tribes were isolated and therefore appeared out of touch. In the modern world, people, most noticeably young people, find an identity for themselves by creating shared and distinctive conventions, that in a sense substitute for the community roles of the old geographical tribes. Cyberspace extends these neo-tribes in new ways: someone can completely and immersively participate in a tribe inside cyberspace, yet even that person's close family or physical neighbours have no knowledge of their other life. Nobody comes and knocks on the door wearing the same sort of clothes. Instead, the neo-tribe member wears distinctive cyberspace 'clothes'. They may feel less understood in the real world than they do with their friends in cyberspace who all, apparently, understand each other. Like everything else to do with people, if the communities people find in cyberspace are supportive and constructive, they become a lifeline and an excellent resource; on the other hand, if they are negative and isolationist, they can become very destructive. Examples of the two extremes would be mutual support groups for people with medical conditions, and, at the other end of the scale, racial hate groups.

In cyberspace we can choose our 'neighbours' – those we bump into in the course of living. This is good, because we can find sympathetic support and expert advice. For example there is a cyberspace group for people with knee injuries, who exchange medical insights, comfort and understanding. In the physical world, however, we have much less choice about our neighbours, whether this is in our churches, in the pub, or with neighbours living on the same floor. Neighbours in real life are alive, and can disagree more readily, and have needs.

Unfortunately, the ease of finding people via the Internet who have common interests and agree with each other makes it easy for them to imagine that more of whole world is like them than is the case. In consequence their thoughts and actions can have a spurious validity.

Data shadows and eclipses

As more and more personal information is available and accessible online, it can be easy to forget that data describe actions or parts of people, rather than inanimate objects. For the people working with personal information about others – in marketing, planning, research, security, etc. – there is always the danger of sliding from describing what people do, to imagining that is what, and all, they are. This is called 'objectification' because it changes perceptions of people from individuals, with the capacity for change, into objects. Politicians have used this process to turn others into enemies or to exclude people from an in-group. Overcoming the dehumanizing features of objectification is one central aspect of the Christian gospel, which offers the hope of a full realization of our humanity.

The problem arises when there is a temptation to treat other people impersonally. Treating people as abstract data objects is just one way of doing this. Data can 'eclipse' the real person, and then decisions may be made about him or her which are inappropriate. Unfortunately, computers happen to encourage this treatment – it is all data to them – so that reliance on them can provide the subtle basis for a 'slippery slope' that eases relationships into the automating and dehumanizing sort.

A large company can use computers to keep track of all its customers. Naturally the company does not want to confuse one customer with another, so each will have a unique identification, usually a serial number, and often supplemented by other information such as postcodes. Now you can ring them up or visit a branch of the company, and within seconds they know as much about you as if you were an old friend.

What goes wrong is that the person working for the company may not have the real freedom to treat you like an old friend. Imagine going to the bank to ask for a loan of some money. The bank clerk knows your name, and maybe asks about your family, even your health. But they can't give you a loan, because the computer has been programmed to treat everyone in a certain data category the same way. Somebody in head office decided that people like you were bad risks, and the computer enforces this blanket decision. The bank clerk, who a moment ago seemed so familiar and affable, is now powerless to act like the friend he or she seemed.

The advantage for the bank is that their business becomes more predictable. At head office, they are interested in the statistics of millions of customers, not in the needs of any one individual. Also, by programming the computer so that the decisions it makes are beyond the clerk's influence, they can run their bank with less skilful clerks who can therefore be paid less. There are more reasons: if the company has enough customers, even tiny gains will add up to significant savings for the company as a whole. Most of these tiny gains will come about by avoiding special cases, so simplifying the company's procedures (as well as their staff training). Large companies have always been able to do this, but now small ones can too, and staff find that the consequence of the introduction of computers is the removal of discretion over their decisions. The result is that relationships are altered, for they are now based on particular categorizations of data held in the bank's information store.

It is surprisingly easy to categorize, and subconsciously relate to, people on the basis of a prior assessment. You read the description of a person and think you know what he or she is like, but they may turn out to be very different when you meet – even a full curriculum vitae gives little indication as to what the person is like. Your surprise on meeting demonstrates that you have already formed some sort of image of them. There is probably a good reason why human beings needed to develop that capability in a large society – quick judgements could be made about who would be reliable, likely to return favours in survival conditions, or prove to be a competitor. The 'natural man', to use St Paul's expression, does indeed classify efficiently and quickly on the most slender of information. For example, since it is unlikely that someone from a competing tribe in the Middle East (say a Samaritan) would help a Jew in need, it makes some kind of resource-efficient sense not to help them – indeed to treat them as 'other'. But these expectations do not exhaust reality, since the guess may be wrong. When confronted by an 'other' who *does* help, or who needs help, we are called to act as neighbour to them (Luke 10.30 ff.) – to change our attitudes towards them, to transcend our own prejudices and guesses about them.

The point is that in cyberspace, people will leave an accumulated 'data shadow' behind them, but however complete it is, it is still an incomplete picture of the person. Since the temptation for those who have access to the data will be to use it for some purpose, say marketing or some other consumer activity, or for political decision-making, they will ignore the differences among those whom they choose to group together. This could easily reflect a false understanding of people and their situation. The question which needs to be asked is: what is the appropriate form of power relationship when people deal in the personal information of others, and can affect their lives?

The power of information

Information is seen to be good and useful in many areas of life. But it can change relationships between people and between organizations, and has already done so.

Doctors in the USA have complained that patients are coming into their surgeries with amazing knowledge of all the latest research, the effect of all the possible drugs to do with their illness and information on who the top specialists are. They have obtained all this information from the web. The doctors say they feel somewhat diminished because they do not have the time to do the same for all possible diseases. The patient–doctor relationship is changing.

Another example is the use of satellites. Coffee-growing Third World countries could rely on some good years of crops to balance bad years' revenue. This was changed when the richer buying countries (primarily the USA) monitored the growth of the crops by satellite and therefore knew whether or not the crop was going to be plentiful. The price of forward buying was lowered and the Third World country received less revenue. And all this happened without the country even having access to the very same information about how their crops were doing. The relationship had moved and the producer was disadvantaged. This is a good example of the point of the phrase 'information is power'. Of course, satellite pictures are also used for other reasons – finding people and areas affected by the Honduran floods, observing what was happening in Tiananmen Square and feeding it back to the reporters on the ground in China for them to do their TV news reports when they were excluded from the Square, and in scientific research on our changing climate.

Who has the power?

Technology is sold on the basis that we can do more and accomplish more with it – in other words it increases our power. Although it does that, we often end up feeling the victims of the decisions of others, often those who seem to accumulate some form of centralized power. Who has the power?

Technology has the power to change relationships between people. It is not neutral. Not all technological products change relationships between people – a new kind of lightweight plant holder might be an example – but others certainly do; a person holding a gun has already changed relationships, irrespective of its use; a national leader holding biological weapons has also changed relationships.

Since cyberspace is all about collecting, analysing and correlating, communicating and storing information, it is squarely in the arena of relationships and creating new possibilities. Cyberspace technology is not neutral. For when computers are introduced into the social context, they alter possibilities – often to the advantage of some and the disadvantage of others. When they are actually being used, they may be seen as bad or good, often both at the same time. Although it would be convenient to be able to describe one technology as good, another as bad, this is not the case. Their introduction shifts power and changes relationships between organizations and people in many different ways, and one of the effects has been to concentrate power in the hands of fewer individuals or organizations.

Lock-in and monopoly power

Computer systems are built on standards. Networks work because the computers on the network speak the same language. Programs work on your PC because they all use a common set of facilities (such as techniques for drawing on the screen, or accessing files). Programs that display pictures work because they all agree on ways of encoding a picture into digital form. You can send a document to someone else because both parties can agree on how the document is encoded. And so on.

For any one purpose at any one time there is usually one dominant standard. It generally emerges out of a ferocious tussle between competing standards. The 'winner' is not necessarily the best technically, but it becomes the best by becoming dominant. Arguably, the Betamax videotape technology was a little better than VHS, but it doesn't matter now: VHS won, and users were locked in to that standard.

If the dominant standard is 'owned' by one company, either legally or because it has an overwhelming market position, then the company ends up with something very like a monopoly. Monopolies are not automatically evil, but they do have the effect of shifting power towards the monopoly holder, and away from the consumer, because the consumer has less choice of buying an alternative product – they are 'locked in' to the standard. Monopolies therefore necessitate obligations, e.g. of restraint and service, on the monopolist, which it would not have if it did not own the dominant standard. In a city where there are many doctors it may be acceptable for a doctor to turn away a patient, but in a remote island when there is only one, the doctor must try to treat all the inhabitants fairly.

Legal processes in regulating monopolies are often slow, and cyberspace moves fast. Though the US Department of Justice is currently investigating Microsoft for unreasonably exploiting its Windows monopoly, the industry is so volatile that by the time the Supreme Court rules Microsoft might just conceivably be a spent force. One of the difficulties of cyberspace is that, whilst we have centuries of experience to help moderate our perceptions of the rights and duties of ownership of, say, land, there is very little intuitive sense of these rights and duties in the ownership of cyber-property, even though the latter may prove even more valuable.

From a Christian point of view, any ownership is a form of stewardship – with the ultimate ownership belonging to God. Consequently all forms of ownership impose duties.

No one understands it all

Individual persons find the technology of cyberspace complicated and brittle – you get no warning that the hard disk on your computer is about to crash (unlike most mechanical devices, where there is usually some indication), and if it does crash you can't fix it yourself. Surprisingly, even manufacturers of the equipment have the same problem. One example is the fault found in Intel's original Pentium chip maths unit. Despite exhaustive testing, this chip was shipped with a flaw that caused certain calculations to go awry, to Intel's great embarrassment and expense. In this case, the flaw could at least be identified and definitively fixed, but software is harder to get right. Even a home computer is now so complicated inside that literally no one can be sure that its software is completely flawless – on the contrary, everyone knows that they are full of subtle flaws, or 'bugs'.

Such complexity can mean people feel alienated from the tools that they use every day, working 'superficially' from outside the box. If we allow alienation to frame our thinking, then it is not surprising that many abandon demands for improvement, leaving it optimistically to others, perhaps even fatalistically disbelieving that change can be initiated. The way a program looks and the way it works are almost completely unrelated. Unless we pore over specialist guides, the way it looks is the main guide to how well it sells – and people only find out how well, or badly, it works after they have bought it. There may be no practical way of finding out whether the insides of the box, i.e. the hardware, the programming and their interactions, have all been done properly. At present the laws protecting the customer which state that products sold should be 'fit for the purpose' have not been found to be adequate to protect them over the purchase of software.

What is a person?

If you send an email to an address that doesn't correspond to anyone, then you may well get a message in reply that says: 'I don't recognize the address bill@wibble.com. Here is a list of six people that you might have been trying to write to: . . . Please do not send me a thank you message; I am a robot and would not know what to do with it.' The 'robot' in this case is a fairly simple program that looks up local email addresses that are similar to the erroneous one you specified, but the message is written as if it came from a person.

This trend is certain to continue. As you navigate round cyberspace you will meet a variety of 'agents': software programs that interact with you. The 'agent' metaphor is a powerful one. There are already whole conferences about software agents (just programs, remember) that are supposed to wander around the Internet on your behalf looking for (say) a good airfare, or a paper you want.

These agents are going to become increasingly lifelike. In virtual reality systems it will appear as though we are able to 'see' them. It is quite possible to imagine that it will become very difficult (or even impossible) to distinguish an agent from a person in cyberspace. That prospect seems to raise a series of questions about what it means to be 'a person' at all. If a sufficiently complex and sophisticated computer program really was indistinguishable from a person in cyberspace, should we treat it as a person? Should it have 'human rights'? Should it be considered an individual before the law? These questions concern our perceptions of these cyber-agents. They might provoke us to ask a different question, though: **in what senses (if any) are humans different from computers?** Such a question may seem fanciful, but we ask it utterly seriously. In 1999 there are no computer programs that can make even a tenuous claim to having the character of a human person – there is little danger of confusing a police constable with a personal computer

– but in 2050 there almost certainly will be. Just as genetic research has increasingly raised serious questions about what it means to be human, so cyberspace is now beginning to do so too. Our brief discussion here will do no more than skim lightly over some very deep water.

Impersonation

The famous British computer scientist Alan Turing suggested the following thought experiment (although we have updated it a little). Suppose you met someone in a virtual reality world. You had extended conversations with this person on each of your visits, you shared your hopes and fears with him or her. Over a period of months you felt that the person became a friend. Now suppose you discovered that this 'person' was actually a computer. No human being was the source of this 'person's' conversation. What would you say? That the computer had tricked you? Or that the computer had become a person, had really become your friend?

Stripped to its essentials, the question is this: if a computer were indistinguishable from a person to us in cyberspace, should we not consider it to be a person? If it walks like a duck, and quacks like a duck, isn't it a duck?

Well, not necessarily. One possible counter-argument is that Turing's thought experiment is a 'set-up'. It is limited by being in cyberspace. We meet almost all our human friends in the flesh, and squeeze their hands. Even those we don't meet, we believe that we *could*, in principle, meet 'in person' (a telling phrase, that means to be physically present). In cyberspace a computer lacks a body for us to relate to, but of course in our cyber-relationships we don't relate to humans through actual bodily contact either. However, if we 'met' the computer which was running the cyber-agent program we wouldn't think of it as a fellow human at all! But perhaps that is because we expect it to look like a computer and not a human. What if computers could impersonate humans *very* well?

A second response is to take this thought seriously, but then say that the ability to impersonate someone perfectly does not make you into that person. Suppose that you meet two identical twins. One of them committed a murder, and one did not. Neither has an alibi, there were no witnesses, and forensic tests cannot tell which of the two was the culprit. The fact that we cannot tell which one is to blame does not change the fact that one is a murderer and one is not. By analogy, it seems that the ability to impersonate a kind of thing (such as a human being) does not necessarily make the impersonator a human being. It is clear that a program's ability to appear to be a person does not necessarily imply that it is a person.

What it means to be human

So it is not enough for a computer to appear to be human, no matter how perfectly. What is enough, then? We may imagine the poor computer asking: I (appear to) think like you, I speak like you, I (appear to) love and hate like you; what else do you want before you call me human? We do not ask these questions facetiously: they force us to ask what it means to be human. We might answer by suggesting some characteristics that humans have and asking if computers can have them:

- Humans think.
- Humans exercise judgement, creativity, intuition.
- Humans love, fear, laugh, celebrate.
- Humans have free will.

So could any of these things be true of a computer, in principle? Here are some common reactions.

- *'Computers are, and always will be, subhuman.'* Computers are built by humans, and they are, at least in principle, well-understood bits of machinery. It is possible to argue that no computer program can embody all the reasoning that humans use, even to establish something as clear-cut as mathematical truth. Thus computers present no theological challenges in principle.

- *'There's practically no limit to what computers can do.'* Computers are getting faster and more powerful all the time; moreover new techniques are being discovered and used. Our human brains are restricted to being inside skulls, and there is no easy way of enlarging them – unless we start supplementing them with computer implants. In contrast, computers can be made pretty much as large and complex as we wish. Size and complexity do not necessarily imply human-like qualities, but they certainly make them somewhat less implausible. Computers already surpass us in some ways (such as calculation); more sophisticated computers will presumably surpass us in more ways.

- '*Theoretically, we can't tell whether computers could ever be persons, but humans are very complex.*' Present-day computers are very simple when compared with human brains, and robots are trivial compared with animal bodies, let alone human bodies. This point of view argues that humans are so vastly more complex than anything man-made that there isn't an issue to worry about.

- '*Computers and humans will converge.*' Thus, the question whether computers are like humans is irrelevant. As computers get smaller, they will simply be embedded inside humans, and computers-and-humans will be a close partnership. Both humans and computers, on this view, will be improved. For example, humans will then have direct access to cyberspace just by thinking about it. (We shall explore this point of view more fully in Chapter 6.)

- '*Most computers don't work very well even to do quite simple things, so it's just silly to ask whether they will ever outshine us.*' Most word processors and video recorders are far too complex, and the millennium bug is going to put an end to our infatuation with computers. There is so much to fix that whether humans and computers are similar is so far off it is merely a theoretical question.

- '*It's too frightening to consider seriously.*' For many people it may be uncomfortable to consider that computers are in any way similar to humans. It is easier to carry on without considering the issues, or to deny there is an issue. Technology will advance, in whatever way it does, regardless of what we think or might want.

One of the difficulties here is that any sort of detailed answer has to delve into what exactly is meant by (for example) 'think', and 'computer'.

Take the question of 'thinking'. A few hundred years ago, most people thought that arithmetic was a skill that required thinking, but today doing arithmetic merely requires a cheap calculator, which no one would say thinks. Computers can play chess very well indeed by the 'brute force' approach of exploring all possible outcomes of a particular move. The result certainly looks like thinking, but is it? If we are not careful we can fall into the trap of using 'thinking' to describe what humans do and computers don't, which rather prevents us from ever classifying computers as being able to think! On the other hand, as we have already argued, merely looking as if you think doesn't necessarily mean you are thinking, as any child knows.

Or take 'computer'. All digital computers are the same in principle, in the following sense. At any moment it is in a particular state. In each time step it moves to a new state, based on (a) its current state (including its program), and (b) its external inputs. From any given state and input there is only one possible new state, so its operation is entirely deterministic. Many people (although not all) would conclude that such a computer could not possibly have free will. (Although that judgement depends on what is meant by 'free will', which is a philosophically disputed matter.) Many people are working hard on so-called *artificial life* and *neural networks*, both of which are innovative ways of programming traditional computers in such a way that the program itself can 'breed' or 'learn'. Computers programmed in this way may well behave in interesting, surprising and unpredictable ways, but they still obey the same model as before: moving from one state to another in a deterministic way, based on the external inputs. How can a computer be both deterministic and unpredictable at the same time? A deterministic computer's behaviour is always predictable *in principle*, but in practice its program may be so complicated that it may *appear* surprising or unpredictable to a human observer. The whole point is that computers running such programs may appear to learn or even to exercise free will, but in fact they are simply following a deterministic program. That is not to belittle them: such programs are marvellous; it is simply to say that they are not doing anything fundamentally different, in principle, from a word processor.

Other people are working on computers based on very different principles, notably *quantum computers* and *biological computers*. Such computers might differ from present-day computers, in the sense that they cannot be described by the state-to-state transition mechanism we sketched above. At the moment such computers are still in the very early stages of development and are far from being in a usable form. The point is that we don't know what sort of computers we will have in the future, so it is hard to say for sure that some future computer would not (say) have free will, even if we believe that current computers do not.

The criteria we have been considering form a set of varied features which we might point to if we were asked to say what were the characteristics of human beings. We have acknowledged that the precise meanings of them – thinking, for example, or free will – are the subject of philosophical controversy, as are the arguments to the effect that nothing which could properly be called a computer could possess free will. Even if these controversies were to be resolved, though, a further question remains. One criterion that a Christian might want to add to this list of what it means to be human would be of quite a different order. This is the affirmation that humans are created, chosen and redeemed by God. This characteristic is not based upon any of the characteristics listed above (thinking, free will, etc.). Unless God had created human beings in the way he has, they would not have possessed these characteristics anyway! So we need to ask: what would computers' possession of these characteristics mean or imply for their relationship with God? And that is not a question that we have any ready means of answering.

Why does this matter?

Intellectual arguments have an important place in Christianity, although not of course the central place. Similarly, intellectual arguments about whether or not computers and humans are fundamentally different are important, because if people believe that it is a scientific fact that humans are simply 'computers made of meat', then all sorts of false conclusions may appear to follow. It can seem an irresistible intellectual temptation to think that all it means to be human may be expressed by such beliefs. That might lead to a range of conclusions about the relative value and significance of human life (such as the essential substitutability of computers for humans in any context whatever – say, as friends or as lovers) which ought to be rejected.

But, as we have tried to show above, such beliefs are based on a view of what it is to be human which concentrates on human *characteristics*, and it remains quite unproved whether this is the really significant part of the story. Christians believe that 'what it is to be human' has to take other things into account – relationships, and especially our relationship with God through Jesus Christ.

To summarize, the status of computers, in terms of their capacity to share human characteristics, is the subject of intense debate, and there are powerful arguments on both sides. Nothing is settled, nor is it likely to be. It is absolutely not a settled scientific conclusion that computers and humans are, or will ever be, fundamentally the same, even in terms of their characteristics.

41

That debate will continue. The point of this discussion has been to place that debate in a proper context, and to show the (limited) significance that it has for an understanding of what it is to be human in Christian terms.

Concluding remarks

In this chapter we have looked at the way that the technologies of cyberspace are value-laden and how their use shapes our thinking. They raise questions of truth, relationship, power and personhood. Cyberspace will, willy-nilly, shape our thinking. Rather than allowing it to do so passively, we believe that Christians should seek to play an active role in this shaping process, and thereby influence cyberspace itself.

In order to arrive at a destination, an aeroplane or boat needs to interact with the forces that push on it one way then another; and the same is true in order to arrive at any chosen end for a social system. We have illustrated some of those forces in order that we can choose how to respond. The next chapter looks at possible destinations and the characteristics that Christianity might seek. By doing so we might begin to know how to gain answers to the questions raised here – 'What is true?', 'What are real relationships?', 'Who has the power?', and 'What is a person?' – in cyberspace.

4

Space Probing

Introduction

In the last chapter we discussed three emerging themes: reality, relationship and power. These themes are central in Christian ethics. In this chapter we consider what principles in Christian ethics are applicable to our exploration of cyberspace.

Many of the implications of cyberspace remain unexplored and the future of the technology is unknown. The opportunity to contribute to the development and use of cyberspace is available now. The speed of change need not deter us from elucidating and applying right principles for participation. The liturgy of Christian worship and prayer, offering as it does a glimpse of eternity, lifts us out of the onward rush of technological change and provides a distinctive point from which to discern which of many possible attitudes to technology, and which of its many applications, are the true and good ones. Our challenge in cyberspace, as in all other areas of our lives, is to discover God's will and to enact it.

The Christian story provides the foundation from which to derive principles of action. The story itself invites a response, and the principles suggest what that response should be. First, we shall outline the story; then we shall identify and apply the principles which seem to us to be apposite to our task of probing cyberspace. The chapter finishes with three 'probes' by which to assess developments and uses of the new technology, to assist the thinking of those who wish to participate in it responsibly.

The Christian story

God as creator and origin

In love God creates the world and fashions humanity. God's intention is that humanity should have a loving relationship with him. That relationship is expressed not only in our love for God but also and simultaneously in loving fellowship with our neighbours, both of which imply respect for the creation by which we are surrounded. Our calling is to love the Lord our God with all our heart and to love our neighbours as ourselves. Our God-given free will and creativity are to be used to fashion just, merciful, loving, inclusive communities in harmony with the whole of God's creation. To use Jesus' language, we are called to foreshadow the kingdom of heaven here on earth.

Human disruption

The call to fulfil our destiny in this way is continually disrupted by humankind's insistence on independence from God. From the earliest times people have used their free will and creativity in ways that separate themselves from one another and from God.

God's reconciliation

God became human in Christ, and entered our world of broken relationships, bringing reconciliation, teaching and healing. In a way that transcends time and space, Christ takes upon himself all the evil and suffering there ever was or ever will be, and through his life, death and resurrection makes it possible for these barriers between us and God to be transcended. By this act, God enables us to live in a full loving relationship with him and with each other, in and through Christ. Our isolation and fear are thereby overcome as we are called into mutual dependence, giving and receiving forgiveness. The amazing love God has shown in Christ demands that we abandon our self-centredness and help those in need. Only thus can we live the full life to which God calls us.

Christian response

From these observations of the Christian story and tradition we can identify the following principles to govern our attitudes and actions in cyberspace.

- *To acknowledge that God is ultimately responsible for what happens on earth.* No part of creation is outside the care and concern of God, including cyberspace. His purposes will be fulfilled. Nevertheless, having been granted free will, humans can act in history and are responsible to God for what happens in their sphere of activity. Christians are called to work actively towards 'Your kingdom come on earth, as it is in heaven'. Our duty, then, is to meet the needs of society and work towards a just and peaceful world.

  Even though God gives us status as co-workers in our spheres of activity, he is the one who is ultimately responsible. Along with the task of working, he gives the strength and ability, through the gift of the Spirit, to accomplish that work. Recognizing this obviously prevents pride, but it also prevents fear: fear that the task before us is too great to be able to achieve. The temptation to avoid working towards God's kingdom, on the grounds that it is too great a task, is surrendered to Jesus' promise that his burden is light. Our engagement with the needs of society is not intended to weigh heavily on us. We do not have to be overwhelmed by the burden of responsibility bearing heavily on our own shoulders; we take responsibility, but as co-workers with God. Nor need we fight evil on our own; the gospel declares that this was done on the Cross. We remember too what the apostle Paul was told: 'My grace is sufficient for you, for my power is made perfect in weakness' (2 Corinthians 12.9 RSV). We can, therefore, move forward with confidence and without fear into the future, including the future that is cyberspace. It should be the joy of love that motivates, not the fear of catastrophe.

- *To live in a spirit of grateful love:* 'Blessed are the merciful, for they shall obtain mercy' (Matthew 5.7 RSV). Christians must be willing to accept help from unlikely sources and to give help, wherever it is needed. We should be glad to be alive. Our actions should be a joyful response to overwhelming love, not a depressing obligation, nor aimed at our own salvation.

Reconciliation takes place between people in forgiving relationships. Cyberspace contains vast quantities of information about individuals. To step free from the constraints of the past is harder when it is on record and accessible to others. Nevertheless the moulds into which information in cyberspace may have put people are inappropriate to proper relationships, and they have to be put to one side in our dealings with each other.

● *To be inclusive.* Jesus particularly attended to those people who were excluded by the Jewish law, bringing them into a new community, and rejecting none on the basis of his or her past if they were willing to accept his teaching. 'Blessed . . . are those who hear the word of God and keep it' (Luke 11.28 RSV). Christians are called to be willing to give up false ideas of who is inside and who is outside. 'There is neither Jew nor Greek, there is neither slave nor free, there is neither male nor female; for you are all one in Christ Jesus' (Galatians 3.28 RSV). In time this became one of the most evident marks of Christianity to others.

It follows that if cyberspace becomes important to living, we should worry about any who are excluded by circumstance or access. The potential that cyberspace offers is closed to those without access. It is like an exclusive club, barred to those without the means of entry, the very opposite of Jesus' intention. The law has enforced inclusivity in the past, for example by ensuring equal access to communication through the postal service, to information about civil rights through local social services, and to books for participation in social democracy through local libraries. Each of these services is proffered recognizing that social inclusion necessitates universal accessibility with low entry cost. The same need is there for cyberspace, if it is to be the means of communication and the source of information for the future.

● *To recognize human frailty.* Human beings share their troubled temporality and finitude with each other, including uncertainty, not being perfect, falling ill and dying. Recognizing these brings humility and forbearance. In cyberspace humility and forbearance show themselves in patience with others struggling to use email appropriately, and in compassion both for those refusing to engage with cyberspace or play a part in it, and those who find it exciting and life-transforming.

On the other hand, the recognition of frailty brings careful consideration to what actions are appropriate in cyberspace. Email allows those with the fragility of warped minds to meet and so find recognition, for example paedophiles. As a result they might not see their own fragility, only their discovery of one kind of (wrongly perceived) normality among others. Frailty is not to be blindly accepted but weighed. 'Whoever receives one such child in my name receives me; but whoever causes one of these little ones who believe in me to sin, it would be better for him to have a great millstone fastened round his neck and to be drowned in the depth of the sea' (Matthew 18.5-7 RSV).

- *To work through inquiry and consent.* God does not force people into belief. Free will is shown not only in human action but also in our recognition of God. In many crucial scenes in the Bible, God manifests his deepest knowledge of humanity by inquiry and consent. He offers, and human beings have the possibility of rejecting the offer. God asks Mary, for example, through an intermediary, for her consent to his divine purpose of Jesus being born through her. Pilate is given a choice about if and how he will deal with Jesus when the religious authorities trump up a charge against him. Even at this extraordinary point, Pilate is honoured by being given the freedom to choose.

  It is this freedom that human beings are called to pass on to each other. Wherever freedom is denied by force or by the misuse of information, humanity is denied. In cyberspace, this is easy to do inadvertently, for example, with data records of individuals. For that reason, UK legislation demands that collection of personal information is signalled to the person, and the opportunity is offered to opt out of having one's details passed on to other companies. These are not very successful attempts to protect individual autonomy, but they are a recognition of the need to do so. The principle reflects God's relationship with human beings.

- *To grow into fullness of humanity.* By the Holy Spirit, God lives and acts in and through believers, giving them power beyond their own (Romans 8.9-14). In this way they know a new level of love, joy, peace, patience and self-control (Galatians 5.22).

47

So much of cyberspace appears to challenge the qualities described as the fruits of the Spirit, such as gentleness and forbearance. For example, cyberspace offers the possibility of desires being fulfilled instantly, before we have the opportunity to exercise the restraint on personal desire that Christian ethics demands. Then, poor interfaces, low batteries or slow communications (relatively speaking), become frustrating and give rise to harmful speech or writing. The nature of the medium of cyberspace may discourage consideration of the effects of our actions on others, when we are miles away, linked only through digital signals rather than being face to face. The fruits of the Spirit may seem far away and difficult to express meaningfully. Nevertheless, Christians are called to recognize that fullness of humanity includes showing those qualities, even in cyberspace.

- *To rejoice in fellowship and interdependence with each other:* to find each other the source of joy (Philippians 2) and its corollary, *to grieve where there is loss of fellowship and relationship* and therefore to have a desire for peace and justice throughout the world, and to work towards that. Cyberspace can be used to magnify these principles of action, or it can be destructive of them. Email has been used to build up friendships and to break them down, to serve justice or to harm it.

The continuing story

The above principles of action are intended as a guide to a proper use of and participation in cyberspace. It is important that everyone who participates does so responsibly, seeking to discover what it means to be fully human in cyberspace as in all other places where one walks and works. But everyone will have and play different roles in cyberspace. Christians will not make a stereotyped response to the issues they find in cyberspace any more than they have done in other places. Some might use the Internet to help release political prisoners, others to worry about child pornography, and yet others to create small, local support networks. The reality of being human means being situated in the world as it is, so that changes to that world, such as the development of cyberspace, affect everyone. There is not one answer to the question of how to participate responsibly in cyberspace, but many, just as there are many ways to live in accordance with God's will.

Probing

To consider intelligently our participation in the continuing development and use of the technology of cyberspace, we suggest three 'probes'. By *probe* we mean, as with its use in electronics, a device for measuring and testing. The probes are presented as questions to be asked as the new technology develops and is assimilated into practice. The questions should be relevant to anyone who wants to use the technology responsibly, regardless of their religious or moral basis.

● *Whose problem are you seeking to solve by the new technology? Will it be solved by it?*

Email has become a vital tool for collaboration and information sharing. We could not have written this book without it. But many organizations embraced email because it promised an end to unnecessary paper memos. The problem of using too much paper was (purportedly) dealt with, but the reason for sending memos was not removed by the introduction of electronic communication. Now, because of the ease of using email, many more memos are sent and copied by, for example, staff who remain as anxious as ever to justify their actions in others' eyes.

● *Will your use of cyberspace bring new, unscaleable problems that outweigh the opportunities?*

It might be good that elected politicians can receive email from their constituents, but at present they can handle the amount of mail they receive only because there is not too much. What will they do when they get thousands every day expecting replies? (That was the experience of members of the US Congress when they were debating whether to impeach their President.) Another example was of a boy who was dying of cancer. Members of the public were encouraged to send him emails, which they did, from all over the world. The tens of thousands of messages he received rapidly became meaningless and impersonal. The ease of communication devalued it.

The year 2000 bug is another example of new technology bringing its own problems. It could have been anticipated and dealt with much sooner. But the cost of rewriting software and changing hardware when the technology to deal with the date change became available seemed too great.

- *Are your problems important?*

You cannot find real food to eat or water to drink in cyberspace. Simple survival is the most pressing problem for the majority of humankind. In this perspective, computers and the self-fulfilment they might bring to their users seem trivial and selfish. Interest in the common good should take priority over individual goals if they ignore the rest of creation's needs. Nevertheless, cyberspace can play its part in serving the common good, and this can be discovered and used to the full.

The issues these probes measure and test are related to human frailty. It would be convenient to focus on human wickedness in some clear and abstract way as the source of the problem, so as to name and articulate it, and then deal with it. But it does not show itself like that. We can no more focus on human wickedness in the abstract that we can give moral evaluations of technologies in the abstract. Instead, we must look at technology as part of the continuing human story of which our times form one small part.

Concluding remarks

In this chapter we have sought to provide a grounding for practical principles to guide our participation in cyberspace. We have made some fundamental observations about the nature of God's creation and his reconciling work in Christ. On the basis of those observations we have drawn up a list of guiding principles to govern our attitudes to and actions in cyberspace. We have applied the principles to some cases. We have ended with three probes to assist the serious cybernaut who wants to participate responsibly for the good of all.

5

Relationships in Cyberspace

The nature and quality of human relationships are of concern to Christians and non-Christians alike. How will cyberspace change those relationships? In this chapter we examine the impact of cyberspace on friendship, neighbourliness, communities and church fellowship. Cyberspace lacks the ability to connect people physically in time and space, but it is able to provide new opportunities for real relationships. Nevertheless, we need to be aware of its possible positive and negative consequences as we learn how to relate to people in this new medium.

What is happening to relationships in Western societies, and will cyberspace make them better or worse? Relationships have been a major focus of attention among those looking at the impact of new communication technologies. Science fiction, including the book that introduced the word cyberspace, quite often has a rather depressing image of the future of human communication: often it is one of people stuck in rooms unlit by daylight communicating via some kind of screen. That fear can be reinforced by the behaviour of some teenage boys, who behave like that for a time (though most come out of this stage perfectly well). Then we read in the newspapers of a company that offers to analyse all the email messages a person has ever sent and reply in the most likely manner to new messages sent to that person – when that person is dead. On the other hand, the same newspapers describe men and women meeting through the Internet and even marrying. Mothers and fathers keep in touch with their sons and daughters at university through email. So what is likely to happen with relationships?

There is no doubt that some social structures are changing anyway and not just because of cyberspace. The number of families in Europe and USA with children and their two parents staying together is declining. There are more people living on their own, or as single parents. There are more old people, especially women.

Where people live is also changing – more are living in towns and cities. It has been pointed out that town and city dwellers see more people in a day than most saw in a lifetime two centuries ago. There is an increasing size of the potential group from which we select friends.

Despite the increasing numbers of people we meet, the number of neighbours we know and number of friends we have has stayed remarkably even. There is more concern over lack of participation in community life, but whether this is due to a shift towards an individualized way of living or technological environment or some other reason is hard to determine.

People have been saying 'Why were the old days so much better?' for at least the last 3,000 years. Were they better? Evidence lends little credence to this view. The writer of the book of Ecclesiastes in the Bible said: 'Do not ask why the old days were better than these; for that is a foolish question' (Ecclesiastes 7.10 NEB). Nevertheless this chapter *will* ask if there is any evidence that cyberspace is changing relationships! We consider in turn friendship, neighbouring and community. We cannot, however, ignore the vision that Jesus offered of a new social structure characterized by complete mutual love and self-giving. Therefore we also consider 'fellowship' – the relationship to be found in church which transcends gender, race, age, class, personality and personal circumstance. Will cyberspace have any impact on this?

Friendship

The number of friends people have and types of friendship do not seem to have changed much over this century. Similar patterns of relationship to those today were evident in 1939; weak relationships were more common than friendships, and people had an average of 13 good friends – similar to today. Interestingly, even in one block of apartments, people said that they knew only an average of two-thirds by name and most not to speak to.

A key feature of the closeness of a friendship is the frequency of contact, and as friendship develops, we get to know more about each other. This is the story of email for many. Two people known to one of the authors got to know each other entirely by email. Then one day the friends (for so they thought of each other by this stage) had a chance to meet, and they arranged an overnight stay. The wife of the host was happy enough at the arrangement, but was a little concerned: how well did they *really* know each other? How would it turn out? It all went fine, but the relationship they had after they had met was different from the relationship through email, for then they knew each other in more 'dimensions' of their lives. Far from the fear suggested in science fiction, it seems that email has become one more method for building and maintaining relationships.

It is possible that some friendships may form and others may decline because of cyberspace. One could wrongly conclude from this experience that somehow cyberspace is changing the nature of friendship, but rather it is that people can now choose from a much wider range of options about how to initiate and maintain friendship.

Neighbourliness

Who is my neighbour? That question lies at the heart of relationships in cyberspace. Traditionally the answer would have been those living immediately around us. They would probably have been similar in some respect – religion, politics or social status – with some of the same concerns – safety against invasion, sufficiency of resources, etc. Unlike friends, we don't choose neighbours – they come with the home, so to speak, rather than the furnishings, which can be changed. In this respect there are many localities in cyberspace where people choose to 'live' (for example in Internet Relay Chat) where their neighbours are not chosen, and who have different ways of behaving and wanting to behave.

The question of 'who' underlies another question: what duties or responsibilities, if any, do you have to a neighbour? The 'who' was the question asked of Jesus when he had said you should 'love your neighbour as yourself'. Jesus extended the localized meaning to include any that we meet in the course of living. Nobody is outside the potential of being a neighbour, although it may never move beyond potential! Jesus' illustrations cover many different angles: the person who needs help, the person who inconveniently needs something from us, the person who helps us. In all these situations our responsibility seems to be to respond as we would have liked someone to do for us (and more).

Some growth of the Internet has been due to people responding to others in such a need – desperate cries for help based around a child's illness or behaviour, or around work needs, as well as much more prosaic cries for help. The willingness of people to respond is awe-inspiring.

Email and other Internet-based communications are perceived as nonthreatening. It is easy to reply, it takes little effort, you are free to ignore messages or responses, and you are not necessarily 'involved' – your response can be limited. You can be a bystander – but no one knows it. In a sense the idea of a bystander is abolished, since no one else can see you not responding; nobody knows you don't want to be involved. In this sense, cyberspace is entirely different from physical presence, when a relationship is admitted, whether a cry for help is heeded or not.

Moreover, another reason for so much help being given is that the scale means that if one in a thousand respond, then that can still add up to a lot of people; many more than is possible in everyday meetings. The potential neighbours are much more numerous and of those a few are willing to help. Again it is instructive to compare the feelings of freedom in cyberspace with those of everyday life. In cities, we meet so many, and so many needs are apparent; 'What change can one person make?' we ask ourselves. The neighbours, to put it bluntly, are too numerous, and we cannot walk away so easily, but nor do we know whose needs are genuine, whom to trust, or how to meet the needs of those we *can* trust.

Community

The nature of community and whether or not you can have online communities has exercised the thoughts of many. Are they *really* communities, or do people just think they are in a community? Are cyber-communities just a sham? And why does this matter anyway? It matters because it affects the way we think about cyberspace, and it matters because calling these cyber-entities 'communities' may change the way we think about what a community could be. Some argue that you cannot call online groups 'communities' because they are disembodied and so the whole rich concept of community is threatened. Some online users claim that they find community in cyberspace, so who has the right to say that they are not in community? And perhaps the debate itself matters because there are many in developed Western societies who no longer feel part of any community and long for it.

Community has always generally been thought of as those people living in a particular geographical space. This means defining a boundary between these people in the community and those who are not. For example, this is the rationale for the political organization of voting in the UK – at least in 1999.

Over the last two decades, the word 'community' has been applied (in an exactly opposite meaning) to particular sections of society – so we speak of the 'gay community' or the 'disabled community'. Partly this is as result of gathering people together for political lobbying and partly it is because people identify more strongly with others with special interests similar to their own if they live in large urban areas where there is more distrust of the stranger.

It is in this second sense that communities exist online, with boundaries maintained on membership and on appropriate behaviour and with representational debate and selection on key issues. People join, meet others, come to know some well and others only by seeing their name appear from time to time in the lists of online communications, argue and reconcile, leave to join another – in fact most of the behaviour associated with other sectarian communities.

So cyberspace is just one of the modern technologies that makes us ask the question: is a community based on geographical nearness now dying? Will cyberspace be another nail in its coffin?

On the contrary, there are examples of the use of online services in the UK, Canada and the USA that facilitate local living. These range from dentists displaying when they have space for appointments, to finding the nearest recycling units and local government information on building proposals. The impact of such modest developments has been described as highly significant because people now feel much more part of the community. It seems that one of the most important features of that is an awareness of what is happening – exactly what would have been communicated through word of mouth when we did meet our neighbours, when we did live in communities.

Clearly a local community should not depend on the availability of IT equipment that many might not be able to afford or be trained to use. But there are also broader issues; for example, the way in which these new techniques may distance people from the decision-making process, turning them into consumers of information, rather than citizens. Such loss of local control appears to be an almost inevitable result of the increasing financial control required locally, and as central government increases its role. The solutions are inevitably political, but individual companies have found that the only way to get through such levels of complexity is to use information technology for access to both information and to people. Thus to care for the needs of the neighbour and the community in this new world requires, we suggest, a political change in how local concerns are handled, with all the relevant information being readily accessible, as it is in the USA, and of course, taking particular care for those without ready access to information via IT.

Church fellowship

For Christians there is another key relationship – that of being part of the Church. How is this different from other relationships? First we want to say that it is not meant to replace any of the relationships described above. The church is not to be a sectarian community, but a group meeting together in faith but also living in the world. Individual churches are *parts of* their wider community, rather than *forming* exclusive communities. So given this, would a cyberspace church be a church?

It is, of course, not the numbers that make the church, but the people. In most churches there is a diversity of ethnic background, age, personality, background and attitude, the like of which is rarely found elsewhere in a society. But a person is not supposed to befriend them all, but to be in 'fellowship' with them. What does this mean? It means mutual acceptance of one another as *children of God*, as opposed to any other part of society and the community, and so living and working out faith together, hearing and doing the word of God. This requires acceptance, seeking the spiritual growth of others, supporting and working together on each other's faith, dealing with negative feelings. There is no choice about fellowship – the Bible commands love, nourishing, sharing and supporting, and so dependence on others to help each develop what it means to be fully human. We might find some also become friends by choice, but fellowship is a biblical imperative.

Expressing things in words is essential to this process of living in fellowship – without the light of language, we cannot explain what is going on, nor how to extricate ourselves from all the habits and ingrained patterns of thought that make us respond in automatic, unreflective ways, hence the traditional disciplines of confession, praise and encouragement. This set of patterns of thought and behaviour that constitute our worship is what Jesus said needs more than words – it needs the Spirit of God too.

In 1985 a new online church was formed on the Internet in which the organizers claimed that for the first time people could worship in spirit and in truth and not be distracted by others who might be 'fat, short, beautiful or ugly. People are pared down to pure spirit.'

What is wrong with that? There is an immediate reaction by many of insisting on the value of physical presence. But then, one asks, what is it about *church* that suggests the importance of physical presence? Superficially it might appear that the closest groups to the new online communities are churches – logging in once or twice per week, participating lightly, having surface enquiries about most of life, perhaps one or two short but deep conversations, and then going away again to live an unseen life for the rest of the time.

If we redescribed church as the place of truth, sought both for individuals and also for what is happening in society, then perhaps that might help guide us. It is estimated that 60 per cent of all communication in a face-to-face encounter is listening with our bodies. That is, we listen to the body language of the other person to understand what they are struggling to say, or to conceal. Moreover, the act of participating in Christian worship is itself physical, in movement, speaking and singing, and taking part in Communion.

This is not, however, to dismiss possible roles for cyberspace; cyberspace can, perhaps surprisingly, be helpful in providing other ways of communicating about our faith. For example, at least one theological college has offered the opportunity for people to send in questions by email, which ordinands then seek to answer, with backup advice and guidance from tutors where appropriate.

Physicality as reality

It's tempting to think that physical meeting is the ultimate in 'reality' in relationships, and maybe that is why some people are worried about relationships in cyberspace. Surprisingly, however, some people are able to be more 'real' about themselves in a letter than in person, so to meet with them rather than have a correspondence with them can be to know them less well. Being physically present with someone can give the illusion that we are sharing ourselves, when in fact all we are doing is sharing some geographical space. Because they are 'there' we assume a communication which has not actually taken place, perhaps through inattention or superficial sociability. Conversely, written communication gives the illusion that a message has been sent and received, when it might not have even been read.

Relationships that exist in cyberspace are real relationships. They often exist solely for the purpose of giving and receiving information, but they can be more than this, like the case of the men who became friends through their email correspondence. For example, they may have asked what each other thought or felt about music or the political situation, about families and about the weather. This is much more than just a reactive response to moves in chess, or a request for information of an abstract kind; it opens up a life rich in realities beyond what we already know.

As humans, we exist in a particular time and place, as bodies which need their physical being affirmed in a variety of ways, through food and exercise for example. If we thought of humans as pure spirits, which happened for the moment to be tied to bodies (as some Greek philosophers thought, but Christians do not), then we might see cyberspace as liberation into true relationships, a glimpse of a higher 'reality'.

It is because of this essential physicality of human being, bound up with our locatedness in space and time, that any relationship that is fully and truly human must be a relationship which exists in and through space and time. The most real relationships between people ought to include, at least potentially, every aspect of human presence, which means that the physical dimension should be includable. Sometimes that is only expressed as a lack, as something missing when we send an email or make a telephone call.

The Christian doctrine of the Incarnation teaches that Jesus was not simply a projection of God into the world, but was really and fully human, and thus able to enter into the world of relationships with those who are fearful or ashamed. Christian doctrine also insists that Jesus will return and fully reveal the kingdom that he proclaimed; a kingdom in which human beings will again relate to him 'in the flesh'. What that will be like, we do not know; certainly the bodily nature of Jesus' resurrection life appears to have been subject to less of what we might call physical limitations. But still it is bodily, bearing the wounds of the Cross, and touchable.

Summary

We suggest that cyberspace is one place that we can use to build and sustain friendships; that it is a place where people can respond as neighbours; and that it can encourage articulation to support and strengthen each others' faith. Aspects of cyberspace certainly reflect the call to respond to the God who spoke and created the world and to Jesus who is the Word.

On the other hand there are limitations to what cyberspace can do. Our existence as physical beings is an important attribute of humanness and not one that Christians believe should or can be ignored. In this sense we share a special relationship with those who live in the same physical space as ourselves, and with the same concerns over what is happening in it. In this sense the Incarnation of Jesus as a fully human being reflects a necessity to attend to those immediately in our physical vicinity, through neighbouring, community and fellowship.

6

Living with Cyberspace

In this chapter we examine some of the ethical implications of living with cyberspace. The list is not exhaustive. We have chosen examples that indicate the range and depth of the ethical challenges confronting us. We look at the impact of cyberspace, present and potential, on business and the world of work; our understanding of property and ownership; our notions of justice when considering, for instance, responsibility for the content of material carried on the Internet; those excluded from access to cyberspace; privacy and the implications for freedom, security and protection of the individual; cryptography and the ability of individuals, groups and the State to keep secrets and tell lies; the integrity of physical beings and the invasion of the computer into our bodies.

How does cyberspace influence the things that matter to us in our daily lives? What are the implications for the world of business and work? Do new questions of responsibility and justice arise? Do cyberspace technologies mean that more people can get hold of our personal details; indeed, are personal details things which can be owned by others, and if so by whom? Beyond these concerns of justice, privacy and so forth, which we see being raised anew by cyberspace, there are questions about the intimacy of our human involvement with cyberspace; for we are increasingly living and relating to one another in cyberspace, and there is even a small but significant trend towards computer implants which might be linked to the Internet.

Business and people in cyberspace

Businesses need to make money – for their owners and for their shareholders – by providing goods and services of a quality and at a price that consumers will purchase. To do this they must operate within the law, which covers much of their actions – financial, employment, product liability, etc. They also have to be competitive in order to survive. If a competitor is using computers, robots or cyberspace to do 'better' in any way, then one is almost forced to adopt these technologies, or see the business die.

Businesses come and go, are bought and sold, expand and contract. The business world is in a constant state of flux, and the advent of cyberspace is greatly increasing the rate of change. However, businesses are important for people: customers, employees, suppliers and shareholders. Businesses are parts of one or more local communities, countries and the global economy. Cyberspace extends the reach and speed of business networking, and hence the impact of business practices on people. Although this book is not specifically concerned with the way in which cyberspace affects the way a business works – many others have written about that – it does need to consider the way in which this new technology might have an impact on working people and their communities.

Globalization

Globalization is having a major effect on product markets and international businesses. Single companies span the planet. Corporate intranets speed internal communications within an organization, while video conferencing enhances professional contacts right round the world without the need for exhausting and expensive physical travel. Remote access (e.g. by email, telephone, Internet and fax) makes it possible for those who happen to be away from their place of work to keep in detailed contact with their base. Call centres handle customer services from any part of the country or indeed the world, speedily and efficiently. And when cyberspace spans the world, it also spans the time zones. A business need never sleep, since it will have wide-awake workers or competitors somewhere.

Globalization can lead to:

● Weaker links between a company and any particular local community, or even country. The UK, for example, has experienced both strong inward investment by foreign companies and outward investment by British companies.

- Weaker links between a company and its employees. There is a danger of employees becoming 'commodities', to be discarded if a cheaper source becomes available. On the other hand, as physical location becomes less important, new job opportunities open up for people in developing countries.

- Unprecedented concentrations of wealth and power. The turnover, and market value, of the world's largest companies exceeds the gross domestic product (GDP) of the world's smaller countries.

Cyberspace did not cause globalization – there have been many other influences at work – but it certainly sustained its growth, and influences its nature.

Electronic commerce

Information technology enables goods and services to be delivered direct to the customer, with deliveries on a just-in-time basis from the manufacturer to an online distributor. This offers real advantages to many businesses, but it has, after all, been here for some years. The really big new change is the development of electronic retail commerce, and that will have many effects on our society. For example, if shopping via the Internet is adopted on a large scale, the future of town centres and other retailing activities might be placed in even greater jeopardy than they already are, for unlike shopping malls, cyber-shopping does not need planning consent! So there is a danger that it will accentuate the problems of inner city deprivation.

Changing work patterns

Information and communication technology has accentuated changes in the organization of businesses that were already occurring. For example, the traditional hierarchical structures within an organization, with clearly defined career progression, are rapidly being replaced by flatter management structures, while networking and team-working, with local devolved decision-making, have become the new, normal style in the workplace. These changes have been of great advantage to the professional worker. They can exploit the benefits of cyberspace, because it can make their work more interesting and more rewarding. This is because their work revolves around their knowledge, skills and access to information, which are then combined to enable them to make judgements and decisions more readily.

One of the key skills of professional groups is 'networking' (in the traditional sense of making contact with others), for which the flexibility and speed of email is ideal. It is no coincidence that electronic mail had its origin in the universities. The ability to 'talk' to one another, to share ideas and concepts, is central to development in all professional areas. Combine email with the web to provide information access, and you have many professionals' dream method of working. Without the restriction of time zones or space for reaching people or information – no closed libraries, no failure to reach someone because they are asleep or away – they work more effectively.

Others have found many opportunities from the coming of cyberspace; they can work from home or from a 'tele-cottage', and are thus enabled to live in rural communities or look after their children at home more easily. But different skills are required; new technical skills and the capability to work away from colleagues and the discipline of the workplace.

As with so many changes, while some benefit, others may lose out through loss of work opportunities. They will require particular support and the opportunity to acquire new skills. But there is another factor at work: the accelerating pace of change in the technologies which support cyberspace, and the expanding range of possibilities for business in cyberspace, may well diminish the need for a stable workforce. More work will be contract driven, and may be performed by freelance consultants. So even the skilled IT professional working on short-term contracts may experience real difficulties over, for example, home mortgages, which are often structured around the expectation of long-term employment. The lack of security may also make it harder to keep local friends and stable schooling for the children. So as work communities become less important, other communities will become more important, and the Church is one such community, indeed the largest voluntary community in any Western country.

Property

Because cyberspace is a real social space, ownership in cyberspace has effects on real relationships of all kinds, and a number of the themes which we have been discussing are relevant to property and ownership.

The easy duplication of objects in cyberspace (computer programs, digital recordings of music or personal information such as health records) implies a need to think carefully about theft, what it is, and why we may be justified in outlawing certain forms of duplication.

The easy aggregation and use of data means that the power of information has greatly increased. We might hardly have thought of a piece of casual knowledge about someone as a 'thing' which we or someone else 'owned'. But substantial 'data shadows' (see Chapter 3) exist relating to individuals and groups; for example, the trading of mailing lists and data records for profit.

The power of ownership of standards raises questions about justice and inequality, at the very least in relation to the market economy. Some standards that enable programs to work together are proprietary, designed and owned by particular companies. It could be made prohibitive for a new company with a good product idea to become established in cyberspace, due on the one hand to the cost of licensing the proprietary standards, and on the other the impossibility of becoming established without access to those standards. This raises questions about the fair use of power.

In the physical world, we have various rules (some with a biblical heritage) about redistributing good things – whether wealth through charity and taxes, or food and other essential items to sustain life. It is obviously bad to withhold the physical necessities of life, and it is obviously bad to mislead people with wrong information (propaganda), but what are our responsibilities over sharing and using information?

The meaning of property

Christian theologians have been more or less unanimous in rejecting the understanding of property that was based upon Roman law. In Roman law, to own something was to have an absolute right to do whatever one wanted with it. Certainly, God has such a right over what he has created; but human beings are to be answerable to God for their use of the good things of that creation. There may be legitimate choices about how to use these good things, but if we use them in ways which serve against the building up of our common life, we are liable to judgement from the one who is the true owner.

Christians have not, on the whole, believed that property is a bad thing. Even though they have a biblical vision and example of common ownership (see Acts 2.44, for example), many of them have nonetheless also justified *private* property. The claim is made that the ownership of property is good; it serves as a basis for personal responsibility and moral growth; it allows us to be co-workers with God in bringing about his purposes. This is actually another way of stating our responsibility to use these goods wisely. Ownership is always relative to God's call on what is owned.

Ownership in cyberspace

This strong vision of responsibility before God is one that we need to translate into the realm of ownership in cyberspace. We may first of all imagine that because life is about flesh and blood, cyber-property must be irrelevant to matters of life and death; but think of the questions of access to your medical records, who owns them, and whether they are available to the right people at the right time to save your life. We may regard the casual copying of some software as having cost no one anything at all, but we should then be reminded that someone has gone to considerable pains to produce that piece of software, and 'the worker is worthy of his wages' (1 Timothy 5.18) – perhaps the only way the programmer can earn money to support self and family.

There are mutual responsibilities here. Charging for a service implies some responsibility, yet software notoriously comes with so-called guarantees and warranties whose only practical effect appears to be the disclaiming of any responsibility. Once you've opened the box, you've paid for it and accepted it, warts (or bugs!) and all, whether it works or not. So manufacturers aren't perfect, as these warranties sometimes explicitly admit. Of course, if a manufacturer wants to stay in business and get a good reputation it needs to develop a reputation for good-quality software, whatever its licences say. The users of the products often don't feel very guilty copying their products when they shouldn't make copies, so they aren't perfect either.

Copyright questions relate not just to the capacity to earn money, but also to the right to take credit for some piece of work, or to publish it. Placing something on a generally accessible web site is placing it before the public, and making it freely available. A first question to ask might be: Is there a right to make this thing public? Has the author consented, for example? There may then be further 'accountability' questions about whether and how we should ascribe responsibility for the content of what is placed on the web. There is heated debate over these issues. When cyberspace had few businesses in it, commercial questions like making money and worrying about copyright were far from everyone's minds. Now profit-making publishers have brought into cyberspace all the conventional worries of copyright and ownership.

Changing perceptions

There are more points that we might make about the changes which cyberspace is making in our perception of the handling of property issues.

New forms of *marketing* are being encouraged by the easy copying of objects in cyberspace. The concept of *shareware* is one where programs (or data) may be distributed freely, and the user is trusted to pay a fee if he or she finds it useful after a trial. The responsibility is on the user to pay, and interestingly users in the United Kingdom seem less likely to do so than those in the United States. One interesting analogy might be with the policy of not charging for admission to a cathedral, but making a suggestion as to the level of donation which would be appropriate. No one is refused admission just because they cannot pay, but there is a recognition that the benefit to those who visit the cathedral has a cost, which those who can pay ought to help to meet.

A variation on shareware is *public domain* software, where the programs (and perhaps the programming code for the programs too) are freely distributed without any cost (apart, perhaps, from a copying fee). The benefits of public domain are that standards are raised, and that people benefit. Public domain material is often the work of large groups of people, many of them experts in the relevant area. Thus public domain software is altruistic, and often of a very high standard because it has been open to public scrutiny. A variation of public domain is *copyleft*, which as its name implies, is an alternative to copyright. In copyleft, the authors assert basic rights to be recognized and allow for the material to be freely copied provided that it is never changed.

New considerations about the pervasiveness of the work of others in what we think of as 'our own work' may make us more aware of our mutual dependence. If I build a web site, it is certainly the result of my labours, but it is equally certainly not independent of the labours of others. My web site may contain material written or designed by other people (such as little pictures); it relies on standards which are proprietary technologies. It may be that the 'work of our hands' has relied on the labours of others much more than we have been willing to admit in the past. Cyberspace might make us more aware of this, and less willing to take all of the credit.

It is hardly surprising that in the realms of property and ownership cyberspace offers both opportunities and dangers. Issues that have been noted are: the recognition of responsibility for authorship; the need of workers to earn a living by the results of their labour; and the power of information conceived as property, both positively and negatively (think of the possibilities raised by ownership of genetic data). Our conclusion, then, is as follows: that ownership in cyberspace no less than anywhere else is subject to the higher claims of ownership that God has on everything that exists, and which implies specific responses to issues of indifference to need, exclusion and exploitation. Right use can be judged by service of the commandments to love God and neighbour, and in the building up of common life.

Justice and accountability

What does justice mean in cyberspace? Here are some examples of situations in which justice may have become blurred in cyberspace, with suggestions as to how a Christian response may help to clarify issues.

Shrinkwrap licences

We have already remarked that software is almost entirely opaque to the user: if it goes wrong it is seldom apparent what has gone wrong, or how to fix it. Despite this, people often have a touching faith in computers. The people who build computers and their software know how misplaced this faith often is! The fact is that large software systems are nearly as opaque to their builders as to their users. They are so big, and so complicated, that usually nobody has a clear idea how they work.

Software is incredibly difficult to test, because it is impossible to try out all possible combinations of circumstances.

As a result, software manufacturers often supply their software with licences that say things like 'For 90 days we warrant that the software will substantially conform to the user documentation', and 'Because software is inherently complex and may not be completely free from errors, it is your responsibility to . . .' These terms are usually accompanied by 'Opening this package signifies your agreement to these terms'. In one sense this is fair: if we use the software we accept the terms, and we don't have to use the software. But the balance of power between supplier and consumer is decisively different from that in other product areas, where manufacturers are held much more directly liable for defects in their products. Is this right?

The Bible says a great deal about the importance of protecting those who do not have the means to protect themselves. The users of computer programs are, arguably, in just that position; not only do they lack power even to identify the true problem, but they are much more likely to blame themselves instead of the product than when they are faced with a defective toaster or car. Yet those same users collectively constitute a market that rewards new features but does not reward new reliability – so it is hard to blame suppliers for emphasizing the former rather than the latter.

Laws (such as the Unfair Contract Terms Act 1977 in the UK) limit the ability of suppliers to impose unfair terms on customers, and there could well be commercial advantages in companies offering better warranties, as used car dealers have discovered. (Unfortunately, in software, unlike cars, there is no obvious way to fix problems. Even replacing software may not fix any problems, whereas – of course – replacing a car fixes at least the original car's problems.) Many businesses have discovered that it is better to anticipate a public desire for more ethical business practices than to take full 'advantage' of limited legal protection. From a Christian perspective there is a strong ethical need to treat the consumer as you would wish to be treated: 'love your user as yourself'. Christian software companies would be hard pressed to reach this ideal, but they might try to think of ways to contribute.

Not shooting the messenger

Rather like the conventional postal system, which transports people's letters around, delivering information in cyberspace requires various intermediary operators. Each operator takes a part in the delivery of messages and the exchange of information. Who is responsible for the content of the information while it is being 'carried'? There has been a suggestion that Internet Service Providers should be made responsible.

In the conventional postal system, the carriers have a special legal status. Beyond the obvious reasonable care they must take, they are not held responsible for the content. It may be illegal to post certain materials (for example, radioactive substances) but it is the people who post them who are breaking the regulations, or the law, not the carriers. There is clearly a spectrum of opinion about what is the right approach, and the legal issues are by no means straightforward. Moreover, laws in different countries vary. For example, in the United States the Freedom of Information provisions ensure that information can be published that is secret in the UK. Or bookshops in Britain can readily stock material that would be illegal in politically more repressive regimes. Or we can write 'Free Tibet' but in Tibet itself people are put in prison for saying so. So even if we decided who was responsible, we have no international agreement about the things which ought not to be done.

All these uncertainties still exist despite postal systems, books, written material and so on having been around for thousands of years! Our society does not seem to know what to do; on the one hand, it wants to make some material judged nasty or secret inaccessible, yet on the other, it doesn't want just to shoot the messenger when the real problems are with either the original suppliers or the final consumers. In the physical world, there is nobody who supports an entirely liberal line that 'anything goes': it is hard to imagine anyone wishing to defend the transport of postcards, magazines, nuclear weapons, venomous snakes or hydrofluoric acid by a public service which treats them all equally! But, in effect, cyberspace currently does just this!

There are obviously good motives for restricting the access of certain groups to some kinds of information. We want to rid the world of torture. There are some people (for example, children and criminals) who are better off not knowing much about it; but there is equally a view that where there is evil in the world, some people – not everybody – should be able to see it and take appropriate action. So it seems impossible that these questions will be answerable by a simple, global solution.

Work towards agreement on standards of professional discretion on the part of Internet Service Providers may offer some assistance in approaching the questions discussed here. These might be – indeed, given the international legislative difficulties involved, might have to be – informally agreed and adopted. They will probably be exploited, but the point would be to make clear where boundaries of responsibility lie.

Exclusion

An underlying theme of much of this chapter has been that of exclusion. The stage effect (Chapter 3) makes it easy to focus on the wishes, needs, interests or rights of those who are part of cyberspace. But what of those who are not?

It is worth distinguishing various different sorts of cyber-exclusion.

- **Badly designed computer systems can disenfranchise their users.** How often have you heard someone say 'the computer won't let me do that', or heard a tale of how a new computer system takes far more work than the paper processes it replaced? The result can be genuine exclusion: people who previously made creative contributions to their work are reduced to human robots.

  This sort of thing may be understandable (e.g. time pressure in development), but it is not excusable. Not only is there no technical or economic reason for it to happen – unusable systems are far more expensive in the end – but such systems devalue people.

- **Cyber-access is expensive for individuals.** Cyberspace depends critically on access to a computer and to the Internet. Whilst neither is very expensive compared to, say, a car or a holiday abroad, both represent an economically significant outlay for many people, and an unattainable one for some. What is to happen to people who simply cannot afford a computer? Are they less important because of that?

- **Cyber-access requires expensive infrastructure.** Developed countries take for granted a reliable infrastructure of telephones and computer networks, but that is not the case in developing countries. There may be some benefit in this; developing nations may be able to skip earlier technological solutions that are now superseded, taking advantage of the economies of scale created by more developed nations. For example, in some thinly populated parts of the world it may be most sensible to use exclusively wireless technology for telephone and computer networks, rather than laying lots of wire. Be that as it may, the plain fact is that a huge proportion of the human population is not remotely connected to cyberspace.

- **Cyberspace is daunting.** For people who have not grown up with cyberspace, it is all pretty daunting. Many people who are not prevented from becoming cyber-citizens for economic reasons are nevertheless discouraged or prevented because they do not have the confidence, skills or access to information and training to begin.

The private car has made many rural bus services uneconomic, and has underpinned the rise of out-of-town supermarkets. Both developments disadvantage those who do not have a car. By analogy, will cyberspace lead to the demise of, say, public libraries? So far, the reverse seems to be the case: public libraries are taking up the challenge of becoming cyber-centres. But the effects of technology are unpredictable, and we do well to be vigilant.

Christians have a duty to speak up for those who cannot speak up for themselves. There is a real risk that those who are excluded from cyberspace will, almost literally, be mute, because they lack the means to speak in the new language. We devalue their humanity, and our own, if we treat them – the majority of the human popluation, remember – as unimportant.

Privacy

We have drawn attention earlier in the book to the fact that computers allow the freezing and manipulation of digital information, and the linking and reproducing of it, on an unprecedented scale. This has considerable and serious consequences. A few examples of the issues that we face give a feel for the implications.

People's emails contain a great deal of a confidential and personal nature. Yet reading emails that have not been encrypted is a straightforward task. In particular, a Service Provider could in principle use people's emails to provide enormously valuable commercial information about them and their companies. The legal status of emails – whether their privacy is protected – remains unclear in the UK at present (mid-1999), though legislation has been promised in this area.

Web sites log the host from which each page was requested, making it possible to identify (by host) who is reading which parts of a site. Matching these data to log-in patterns (or intelligent use of interaction with the host) would allow site operators to track exactly who is looking at which pages. This not only allows (say) an online bookstore to track which books you are buying, but also those which you are considering buying.

Integrating the information from various rich information sources can give a quite precise picture of a person's life. Imagine an integration of bank, credit card, phone, loyalty card and web access information: how valuable to a prospective employer, an insurance salesman, or a thief. It could be wonderfully useful to the Government to ensure information about a citizen is kept up to date with regard to benefits, tax, liabilities. It also raises deep-seated issues about freedom, security and protection of the individual from the powers of the State.

Once a 'digital memory' has been created it has the potential to be indefinitely persistent. At present, it takes somewhat determined investigation to find a youthful indiscretion of a respected public figure, but if every public document (including court records) were immediately available online only a few clicks would be necessary. As a counterpart, digital memory can be erased completely. So cyberspace gives the potential for perfect forgetfulness, too: information could disappear without trace.

These examples imply that developments in cyberspace will have effects on our privacy. What kind of good is privacy? Surely, if God is omniscient, then we can have no privacy before God. A Samaritan woman discerned Jesus' unique status because he 'told me everything I ever did' (John 4.29 NEB). If God already knows all our thoughts and actions, then maybe the privacy that we seek and affirm in others is only a conditional good, appropriate for the fallen sinful world.

However, even if privacy were only a conditional good, because we are sinful, but not of inherent value, there are strong arguments based on the primacy of love for protecting it in other people. The mere fact that someone would be upset if certain personal information were revealed or used is, other things being equal, an argument against revealing or using such information.

There are some other considerations which suggest a more positive connection between privacy and the human condition.

- There is a clear connection between love and the free gift of self-disclosure, made manifest in the Incarnation. It is not an accident that friendships are cemented by confidences and that nakedness between a man and a women belongs within marriage. There are aspects of privacy which enable self-disclosure to be a gift of intimacy, rather than something forced upon us.

- The fundamental importance of personhood in the Christian understanding means that we are never reducible to the sum of the information about us. One of the principal objections to pornography is that it devalues the human by turning intimacy into an image, and makes what should be deeply personal essentially impersonal. Similarly, personal information of any kind is not a freely manipulable commodity, but one which demands sensitivity and respect in its treatment. (Indeed this is a fundamental principle of the legislation governing the storage of personal information in computer systems in the UK – the Data Protection Act 1984.)

Email privacy and logging web access both raise issues of security. We can readily imagine situations where a plausible defence of particular instances of email interception, for example, might be made. We will return to these questions in the next section in this chapter. Web site owners might well justify logging and storing access and activity information in order to improve their service to customers, by providing better or more accessible and relevant material. This justification lies in the benefit to the user, but the user is not being asked what he or she would count as a benefit, and it might well be better if suitable opportunity for feedback (by questionnaire, say) were provided. There are clearly important issues regarding the extent to which this information can be disclosed to third parties. Our view is that there should be a strong presumption of non-disclosure.

With regard to the integrating of personal information, there seem to be two concerns which may arise. The concern of direct abuse of this information (by a thief, for example) is obvious enough. There is a further danger: the fuller the information picture, the 'data shadow', the greater the chance of a person being implicitly identified with that data shadow.

A person is not simply the sum of recorded facts about them, and there could be a danger of 'reducing' our perception of someone to what is recorded about them. This relates to matters discussed in Chapter 3.

The persistence of data presents a genuinely difficult issue. Any derogatory information about someone should only be posted on the web (or otherwise made available to the digital world) with circumspection, and should be removed when it is no longer necessary or appropriate for it to be displayed. Indiscriminate archiving of past information should also be discouraged, irrespective of concerns regarding copyright. Yet such archiving is remarkably simple to achieve, and digital records may be copied to a large number of locations. If someone is found to have been wrongfully imprisoned for an offence, can we be sure that significant cyber-records of the original conviction will all be either erased or linked to the new information of the person's innocence? Caution in archiving is clearly necessary. It may also be necessary to learn how to live in a world that has forgotten how to forget, and Christians may have much to teach about forgiveness.

Retail services are being offered in cyberspace through online catalogues, with the opportunity for customers to make 'virtual inspection' of available products. In so-called 'recommender systems' customers are encouraged to comment on products so that they help each other. This increases customer satisfaction, because they are more likely to order what they want, and because it gives them a real sense of participation. Some suppliers add features that are not possible in conventional mail order: as the online customer fills in their forms, they are told that other people with similar interests also like certain other products, which are then being recommended to the customer. Such systems are often uncannily accurate, and people often welcome their helpfulness, rather than worrying about the intrusion into their privacy.

Why is there an intrusion into privacy? Surely recommending books or sock colours is excellent? Well, yes. But suppose we were at the online pharmacist and ordered a contraceptive, and the system said that similar customers liked to go to such-and-such a doctor, and so on. Here, far more obviously, there are issues of privacy. Also, as the services become more sophisticated, it is clear that the recommendations will probably encourage people to make popular or profitable rather than wise decisions.

Secrets and lies

There is a new technical area which has considerable implications for discussions of privacy. This new area is cryptography, an area that is a lot more extensive than sending messages in secret codes. With recent developments all the following have come together:

- **Untappable communication.** The fundamental thing that cryptography does is to make it possible for a group of people to communicate with each other in a way that is (so far as we know) virtually impossible for anyone to eavesdrop upon. However good they are, ordinary safes can always be opened by using cutting tools or explosives. The new computerized 'safes' are much more secure.

- **Unforgeable signatures.** It is possible to 'sign' an electronic document better than it is possible to sign physical documents. An electronic signature using sufficiently strong encryption techniques is virtually unforgeable, easily identifiable, and it is virtually impossible for the signed document to be changed without the change being detected.

- **Public key security.** So-called public key cryptography permits a range of new ideas. The simplest is that a person (or organization) can advertise their 'public key' (of which they may have several) which anyone in the world can then use to send secure messages back to that person. By using the public key, anyone can 'lock' messages, and only the person who owns the key can decode them.

- **Group security.** Just as conventional safes can be designed so that two or more people must be present to open them, many sorts of group security are possible.

These ideas arose only in the 1970s; new, then, in the sense that cryptographic techniques have been otherwise basically unchanged since biblical times. These new technological possibilities raise a host of political and moral questions, mostly centred on the conflict between individual freedoms and the interests of the society to which we belong.

Anonymity and audit trails

Take electronic cash for example. With digital signatures, it is straightforward to write an unforgeable cheque. More can be done, however. Someone can order goods from a supplier through the Internet and arrange for their payment without any bank knowing either their identity or the identity of the merchant. This is surprising, because the bank has to be involved to confirm the creditworthiness of the account.

There are two conflicting views about cash: coins are very convenient, but they are hard to track; conversely, cheques and other paper transactions are more tedious, but are much easier to track (even paper currency has serial numbers). Individuals prefer the freedom of coins, and organizations and governments prefer the audit trails left by paper records.

The controversy is this: the different sorts of electronic cash can, in principle, be even more anonymous than conventional coins, or on the other hand, electronic cash can be even easier to audit, depending on what 'you' want. There are many 'yous' in this equation: nations want to have more control, banks and commerce want efficiency and profit and individuals want autonomy and trust. Furthermore, the military and secret services are interested, as the technology to do these things relies on various forms of 'secrecy', which is their stock-in-trade.

There are parallel issues with secure voting. Voting is a bit like spending money: you can only 'spend' what you are given, typically one vote; you can only spend it once; and you must be able to spend it anonymously. Also, just as people want to count money accurately, they wish to count votes accurately. So, the issues are technically almost identical.

Big brother is watching you

Governments feel uncomfortable with citizens having essentially unbreakable security. In particular, it is argued that law enforcement agencies must always have a right to access people's secrets because occasionally their secrets are illegal.

This can be made possible but should it be allowed? Let us consider, for example, various forms of key escrow. (Escrow is a legal term meaning something held by someone until some condition is fulfilled, for instance some money may be held in escrow until a child is 18.) The basic idea is that your secrets are really secret to everyone except to suitably authorized people (such as judges, or the police). For anything you decide to lock up electronically, you would be required to lodge a 'copy' of the key in escrow, that is in a secure place that could be accessed in emergencies. This is obviously a good idea if you have sealed your last will and testament, which must only be read when you are dead! But it may not be a good idea in many other areas of life, since it assumes the escrow agency is always trustworthy and works in your interests.

There are some delicate balances to be struck here. For example, there is a difference between giving the police the right to access our secrets if they have justified their reason to collect evidence (say, if they have a warrant), and designing the technology in such a way that the police have a blanket mechanism for surveillance. Even if we have grounds to trust our own police, not all users of the technology might be so worthy of trust.

There are very similar arguments for and against monitoring what is being done. In electronic cash, there is the privacy of the way the individual spends his or her money, against the wishes of the banks or the State to monitor appropriate behaviour. In voting, there is the privacy of the voter's opinions against the necessity of counting votes and guarding against fraud.

Modern cryptographic methods can achieve almost any desired balance of outcomes; what is tricky is deciding what outcomes we want. Amongst all the technical possibilities, there will be ones that suit 'society' more than others; and what suits society may not be what suits individuals, or particular groups of individuals.

Implants: bringing cyberspace inside

So far cyberspace has been envisaged as 'out there', helping run businesses or whatever. But it won't stay like that. The cyberspace that is outside will come closer, and the moral issues will become more pressing.

Most computers we interact with are quite clearly outside us; we talk to them with keyboards and screens. Some people get closer, and wear computers – some wristwatches are quite powerful little computers, and can do useful things. A few people have computers actually inside them: in pacemakers, in hearing aids. Even fewer people already have computers inside their skulls acting as direct brain-stimulating aids to help them see or hear.

If we jump ahead in time, then computers will be inside many of us, as implants. Thus the issues we outlined earlier will also be right inside us. If we are optimistic, this would be a huge benefit; and if we are pessimistic, when computers literally get under our skin, there will be very difficult problems.

At first sight the implant-in-the-brain end of this wide spectrum raises more serious ethical questions than our external 'partnership' with desktop computers with keyboards, where people can always walk away from the computer. Actually, we can't always just 'walk away'; the computer remembers who we are, and a 'data shadow' follows us around for our entire lives. Like it our not, we have a symbiotic partnership with computers. Bits of computers physically implanted within us are just one colour of the broad spectrum of possibilities. However, when computers are inside us, they become part of us, and this part-of-us-ness makes some of the ethical issues seem much starker.

No one knows how far the possibilities of implants can extend. The 'direct interaction' between our brains and a small computer will depend on a lot of work by neurophysiologists. Certain functions of the brain seem to be localized, and perhaps these functions could be enhanced by a computer implant. The chip at the heart of a calculator is about the size of this letter 'o'. It could be slipped inside someone's head and wired up to a few nerves. Such a person could conceivably then do calculations very fast and very accurately. People who are financial traders who rely on fast financial dealings might be the first to sign up: they have the money to buy the implants, and traders are typically 'first adopters' for new technologies – and implant-enhanced traders would have even more financial incentives than most of us to think harder. Or what about artists who crave for creativity and new experiences?

We might ask the question: what would happen if it were possible for a computerized bit of our brain to make moral decisions for us? What would happen if we had implants that gave us direct connection to cyberspace – a sort of cross between a mobile phone and modem in one's head? Would we get lost in cyberspace and become oblivious to our surroundings, in a drug-like hallucination, or would we be become informed, wiser and deeper thinkers because of our wide, human connections?

CHURCH HOUSE
PUBLISHING

and the Board for Social Responsibility invite you to the launch of

Cybernauts Awake!

Ethical and Spiritual Implications of Computers,
Information Technology and the Internet

On Wednesday 17th November between 12.30 p.m. and 2 p.m. at the Church Commissioners, 1 Millbank, London

Copies of the book, published by Church House Publishing, will be on sale priced £5.95

Light refreshments will be provided

RSVP to Margaret Rees, Board for Social Responsibility, Church House, Great Smith Street, London, SW1P 3NZ.

Email: margaret.rees@c-of-e.org.uk Tel: 0171 898 1534

Delegating decisions

Such questions might seem far off into the future, or in the realm of science fiction. But already computers that are outside our bodies make major morally significant decisions. Here are some examples.

- Everyone's credit rating is based on all sorts of factors, which only a few years ago would have only been entrusted to wise and mature people. Now we accept – or put up with – 'mechanical' decisions about whether we are trustworthy. Once bank managers were experienced (wise? old?) people; now bank managers are in their early twenties, making only those decisions that Head Office's computers will let them take.

- Children using the Internet, especially in schools, connect via filters, which are programs that stop them accessing undesirable material. What counts as undesirable is a moral issue, and because people have decided to delegate it to computers, the children probably do not even know decisions are being made on their behalf.

- Prisoners have electronic tags that they cannot remove. These tags may be controlled by (quite simple) computers, which impose society's will on them in a very physical way.

Some people might say that these aren't examples of 'decisions' at all; only people really make policy decisions, and the computer executes them. That's actually disputable; are we speaking literally or metaphorically when we say a computer chess program is 'deciding its next move'? What is clear is that humans sometimes delegate decisions to objects, tossing a coin to decide which way the teams will play in the first half, say. That would be quite a trivial decision, but we could have complex, and obviously morally significant, decisions delegated to computers. The decision to delegate would itself be a moral decision; what would be at stake? We might find that some decisions which we currently agonize over are, one day, routinely taken by computers. Having devolved decisions, and thus perhaps eased the sense of responsibility, we cease to notice the moral dimension at all; issues become 'de-moralized'. Another concern is that our whole vision of the ethical is at stake; what basis do computers make decisions on? Maybe they could calculate consequences of actions better than we can, and some people do think that consequences are the only guide to what is right and wrong, although most Christians have resisted this view.

The point is that, ultimately, these moral decisions could perhaps be delegated to tiny chips embedded inside our head. If it could be done at all with innocuous and useful things like calculators and hearing aids, then it might be no more difficult to implant a credit-rating system inside the head of a bank manager, or even a 'moral filter' inside the head of a child. These acts of delegation raise very major moral questions. But there are other issues.

Some issues over implants

There is, currently, a feeling that a society relying on brain implants would not be a good thing, and we would only like it, if it happens at all, if it had been developed carefully and by small steps. However, commercial pressures may bring it about, whatever we think.

There must be serious questions about whether and under what circumstances it is right to install implants, and they are issues that would be for the surgeon to work through just as much as the possible recipient. They raise moral rather than spiritual questions, but there are also spiritual issues, such as those that would arise if it were possible for an implant to change one's personality. Perhaps you should find out how to use the gifts you have got, rather than want to be a different sort of person! Well, that sounds pretty far-fetched at the moment, but it's not out of the realms of possibility.

Beyond the personal lie social justice issues. Perhaps half the world has never made a telephone call, and those unconnected people are hardly likely to get computer implants. Their lives may not change, then, but the people who do get implants will be 'better' – and the divide between the rich and poor will increase. Implants will doubtless cost money to install, so the rich would buy the implants, but then they would get even richer, thus exacerbating the division.

Currently, enthusiasts are excited about the potential for implants, and few people can realistically benefit from them. Each success will be heralded as a wonderful advance (which some, at least, might be) . . . until one day, implants become consumer items. Perhaps nanotechnology (very small devices) will allow implants to be injected inside us in moments, as easily as we now get a vaccination.

So how can we stop the promise turning into a cause of injustice, discontent or isolation of people who are materially excluded from the wonders of the implant-blessed? Indeed, does the technology improve human relationships in general? We could sharpen this question with a Christian view: that building up our common life is a good thing, and therefore to be prioritized.

Thus the question raises subsidiary questions, some with quite controversial implications. Should there be legislation and regulation? We are already debating analogous questions with cyberspace, limited though it is with today's conventional technology. For example, should the Internet be taxed? Should there be a byte tax? Clearly it would be worth debating these short-term issues with the other, long-term issues in mind.

Deciding what we want

Since many of the issues in this chapter concern the differing interests of individuals, organizations and societies, it is inevitable that legislation and regulation will play an important role. Since legislation is enacted by governments, one consequence will be that individuals' rights will often be balanced against national and commercial interests.

It is easy to imagine that economic or security concerns will dominate (if not in the UK, then they will in some countries) and these concerns may not promote liberty, charity and (for example) easy ways of helping the poor. For example, it could be made illegal to use electronic cash in certain ways and, if so, the computer programs available could make it literally impossible to do so. Because cyberspace is or is potentially worldwide, what we might find acceptable in Britain or in Europe might be unacceptable in other societies, or vice versa, and that raises the need for international agreements which, as we know from our experience with issues such as global warming or biodiversity, are not easy to achieve.

7

Cybernauts Awake!

When astronomers look at distant galaxies they know that they are observing events which happened at least a million years ago. It is inevitable that by the time this book is published some aspects of cyberspace will have changed appreciably. Nevertheless, issues in computing have a longer persistence than is generally recognized – many developments hailed as new and revolutionary turn out to have been around for about 12 years. Thus we have tried to outline some specific implications for the various groups of people that are affected by these developments, and who might be reading this report. The specific groups we have in mind are:

- **Information technologists.** People with specific responsibility for designing, specifying and implementing cyber-systems also have a very specific and deep responsibility for creating the cyber-environment in which we live. Professions such as medicine have vital influence on our lives only at very specific times; by contrast, advanced societies are dependent on cyber-systems on a minute-by-minute basis.

- **Directors of organizations commissioning cyber-systems.** Since information technology professionals are ultimately employed to deliver benefits to organizations, the people who run such organizations (businesses, public sector bodies or charities) have enormous influence over the types of cyber-systems that are created. This influence is not always used consciously or wisely.

- **Users of cyber-systems.** We are all (including, of course, information technologists) in this category in many different ways. Even people at the leading edge of creating new cyber-systems for the most powerful providers of cyber-systems on the planet are (at least) as dependent on cyber-technology as the rest of us. As users we can 'vote with our feet', or increasingly with our clicks.

- **Parents and guardians.** The impact of cyberspace on our children's lives will be even more pervasive and profound than that on our own. What can, and should, concerned parents and guardians be doing?

- **Christians interested in cyber-space.** Since cyberspace changes the way in which we relate to each other it has spiritual implications which Christians may wish to explore.

These groups are not hard-and-fast divisions – people can fall into all five. In the story of the blind men and elephant, each person got hold of a different part of the elephant and concluded that it was very like a snake/spear/tree/wall. The story is mildly amusing because we can imagine seeing the whole elephant, and can easily see how misleading conclusions can be drawn from focusing on only one perspective. But our position in gaining perspectives on cyberspace is that no one can see it all, and it is changing so rapidly that by the time perspectives are communicated and shared they are liable to be out of date. Nevertheless, each set of 'implications' offers a different viewpoint on the rapidly evolving elephant that is cyberspace.

Implications for information technologists

We should be humble co-creators

Despite our limitations, we are co-creators of a new and vitally important dimension of being. Offer it to God. One great idea, well implemented, could make a real difference to millions. One misplaced comma in the software could seriously harm someone's life (it is suggested the Atlantis space shuttle blew up for such a reason).

Love your user as yourself

The user is your neighbour, someone whose true well-being you can materially affect. We must therefore love the user as ourselves. How would I feel if I, my spouse, my children, parents or best friend were on the receiving end of this system?

Good design is a moral issue

Architects in the 1960s and 70s were excoriated in the 1990s for buildings which looked good on paper but which were not easy to live in, and which were made of sub-standard materials. Many of the factors at work then still apply to cyber-systems. There are continual pressures on information technologists to skimp on good design and specification in favour of 'getting the system out'. Such 'economies' are almost never in the interests of the organizations pushing for them, who generally end up paying ten- to one thousand-fold for poor early design decisions. Robust professionalism is important here.

Management projects values

Delivering cyber-projects almost invariably involves a significant amount of stressful work and long hours. IT people are not famous for their high level of interpersonal skills. Nevertheless there is a huge difference between a good and bad climate in the management of a project. Fostering a good climate, where the team feel and act like a team of respected professionals, is likely to result in much wiser and more moral decisions. It is also an important moral duty – your colleagues are your neighbours as well.

See the ripples

Reflect on, and try to understand, the wider implications of your work. This is well worth it – it is interesting, will make you a better professional, and (by the way) will greatly increase your value to employers.

Implications for directors

Your nervous systems interact deeply with your personality

The nature and functionality of the 'digital nervous systems' that permeate your organization profoundly influence the type of organization you are. There are fundamental strategic issues here, which cannot just be left to the 'techies'. Ask yourself: how can we be sure that the systems we implement will help us become the kind of organization we need to be?

Your organization's success depends on the quality of your cyber-systems

In 1999 there was a frenzy of Internet-related stocks in which even soundly based and highly successful Internet-related companies were valued at almost ridiculous levels, and almost any business could be hyped with the suffix .com. This was an overreaction to a fundamental truth – that for many products the web is the primary means of interaction for upmarket customers. Already in 1999 the most important medium for exchange of business information is over the Internet.

Listen to the 'techies' and try to understand them

If you want sound 'nervous systems' constructed then you need to ensure that there is a sound environment in which the construction is taking place. Pressurizing the IT people to deliver according to schedule come what may, regardless of the realism of getting a reasonable system built on time, virtually guarantees poor systems in which the users' real needs are sacrificed to expediency and 'getting the management off our backs'.

Be an intelligent client

Being an 'intelligent client' is arguably even more vital for a cyber-system than for a building, but harder. Smart suppliers of cyber-systems work hard to try to understand, and be seen to understand, the organizational needs which their cyber-systems are meant to address. But salespeople in computer companies get paid a great deal of money, and have sales quotas to meet. There is no substitute for making a real effort to understand what you are being sold. It is also essential to monitor, in a constructive but firm manner, what subsequently occurs. Clients notoriously fail to manage the operation of large systems-related contracts effectively. The persistent success of companies notorious for taking tens (or sometimes hundreds) of millions of dollars from clients to implement systems that do not work and which subsequent analysis suggests could never have worked strongly suggests that there are many unintelligent clients out there!

Implications for users

Vote with your mice

Organizations use cyber-systems in order to get better results. They don't want to implement systems that users hate. Make your views known (a good use of email) and be willing to take your custom elsewhere.

Remember systems are dust

Although anyone who has worked with computers knows how fallible computer systems are, there is still a dangerous naivety about 'the computer says', 'computer predictions' and the like. Not only are there fundamental limitations in principle to what computers can do, but computer systems are also limited by the fallibility and lack of foresight of their human designers and implementers, and by the quality of the data they are fed. One of the oldest acronyms in computing is GIGO, which stands for 'garbage in, garbage out'.

Be empowered with information, not intimidated by it

There is a plethora of information out there. You can use it and make the difference. In so many fields the ready availability of information in cyberspace redefines the balance of power between individuals and large organizations.

Naive computer dependence can be especially dangerous

Even sophisticated users often fail to make regular backups and fail to encrypt sensitive email or take the normal routine precautions that are the equivalent of locking doors and checking that the fire is out. As we all become increasingly computer dependent this casual stance is likely to be increasingly dangerous.

Digital deception is easy – and nearly ubiquitous

A healthy scepticism about digital images and information is increasingly necessary – manipulation that would have been regarded as faking is now routine in many contexts.

Use email with care

Netiquette (email etiquette) is important. Avoid 'flaming' (sending offensive angry emails) or 'shouting' (CAPITALS). Flaming happens very easily in cyberspace, even descending into a flame war. So recognize when people flame and either ignore it or give a gracious reply. It is quite likely that the person you think is being rude had no intention of doing so. Conversely, if you make a joke, put a smiley after it – a sequence of characters like this :-) that looks like a face – so that they won't be upset if their sense of humour isn't like yours.

Implications for parents and guardians

Use cyberspace with your children

The Internet is not a fad, and will replace the telephone as the dominant means of communication in most relationships while people are unable to be within physical earshot. Learn to use this medium – it's tremendously useful, and fun, once you get over the first few hurdles. At least by the time your children grow up and leave home it will be essential in order to keep in touch. The moment your children get online, get online too.

Don't be afraid to learn from your children

They learn so quickly, so have them teach you; and it's fun too.

Be aware of the potential for deception and depravity

Although most of the people who provide content on the web are either commercial or 'innocent', the web can also be used for some of the 'sick' purposes discussed earlier. There is a huge free-speech culture, and in the US provided you are not an anti-abortionist, it seems that you can post anything you like.

Develop some safety rules

The following set of rules for children is based on the suggestions from the excellent organization childnet (http://www.childnet-int.org):

- Always tell a parent or adult if you come across bad language or distasteful pictures or find material which is scary or threatening.

- Always keep your personal details safe and never give out your name, address, phone number or school's name.

- Only agree to meet someone you have met in cyberspace once you have your parent's/carer's permission, and then only when they can be present.

- Take care when chatting to people in a chat room or through email. Never hang around if someone makes you feel uncomfortable or worried.

Consider investing in a filter or control tool

Software is available which can restrict your child's access to potentially unsuitable material. Remember that such software is no substitute for parental involvement.

Stick to the positive

In the same way that you look out for good books or good TV programmes for your children, look out for quality web sites that are specifically written for children.

Know who else to report to

If you come across harmful or illegal material make sure you report it. You can find out about hotlines at www.childnet-int.org/hotlines/

Implications for Christians

Analogies, not idols

Christians may find some encouragement in the development of cyberspace and cyber-concepts. People who once scorned the notion of 'spiritual reality', and who rejected Christianity accordingly, might find their ideas transformed by experience in cyberspace. We should beware, however, of replacing one crass perception of the whole of reality as 'just material stuff' with another of 'just immaterial stuff'! Related to this, we should insist that Christians do not think of spiritual things as being opposed to physical ones. Cyberspace may offer us a rich new store of analogies and parables – 'intelligent agents' in cyberspace may seem a bit like angels. But we must always be aware of the limitations of these analogies, and not become so enamoured either of them or of cyberspace itself that we set up false understandings and false gods.

The gospel is bigger than cyberspace

Historically, every new advance in communication has been a means of proclaiming the gospel, and cyberspace is no exception; cyberspace can be used in the service of the gospel. However, those hostile to Christianity have always looked to the latest developments in any field for proof that the gospel is false, irrelevant or outmoded. Christians will need to beware of such arguments in this developing area, and show up their weaknesses in logic or science.

Add a cyber-stone or two

Putting material up in cyberspace is easy. If every Christian with an account at an ISP puts up some material with explicitly Christian content and links in to other beneficial sites, cyberspace becomes increasingly populated with helpful content. It's rather like adding a stone to the marker cairns on mountain paths – if we each do a bit, the result is significant. Participate in online debates, so that Christian voices are heard. Churches should be very proactive about a cyberpresence: cyberspace is increasingly the most important source of information about organizations. It should be as easy to find out about local churches as local cinemas!

Seek the common good

Cyberspace is a strong force for social change, and Christians should be using it to work for social justice and evangelization. To give just one example, could your church promote socially responsible economic causes through its web site?

Praying for and in cyberspace

For Christians, one way of realizing their dependence upon God, and the characteristic way of expressing their concerns to God, is in prayer. There are a number of ways in which cyberspace can be relevant to our praying, some of them simply useful extensions of our existing means of sharing our needs for prayer with friends. Cyberspace is a place where relationships are forged and sustained. So we need to appreciate that the words Jesus gave his disciples to pray, 'forgive us our sins, as we forgive those who sin against us', form a prayer which, in our own context, applies to cyberspace relationships too. As we pray for healing of damaged and broken relationships, we may do well to extend our concerns towards events and relationships in cyberspace.

The Church is a real community for the twenty-first century

Cyberspace tends to reduce the 'real' contacts that people have at work, and there is a risk that workers in cyberspace become increasingly remote, and that is increasingly important in our fragmented world; gathering people together in real communities becomes an increasing human necessity. For twenty centuries the Church has been serving in this way, and it will go on until the end of time.

We are tremendously excited by the opportunities of cyberspace. From papyrus onwards, every major development in communications has provided new channels through which the gospel is proclaimed. Cyberspace is no exception. So many people are kept away from the Christian faith by fear, ignorance and oppression. As cybernauts awake we will continue to rejoice in the amazing news of the Word made flesh. Heaven, earth and cyberspace are full of his glory.

Appendix

Annotated Bibliography

This annotated bibliography contains books which have been formative over the years or which have been particularly helpful in writing this report. Thus it is not intended as a general introductory guide to the literature available, but is instead more for those who want to follow up some particular aspect.

There is, of course, a difficulty over the dating of books written about technology. We have chosen books containing ideas that do not date, even though some of the illustrations might be old.

Books on technology and its place in society, from a Christian perspective

Perhaps the most substantive Christian thinking on technology can be found in *Responsible Technology*, edited by Stephen V. Monsma (Eerdmans, 1986). This is a substantial book intended for the general reader. Some familiarity with sociological language would help in reading it.

A very readable introduction to general technological issues is *Human Future? Living as Christians in a Hi-tech World*, by Alan Jiggins (Scripture Union, 1988).

General books

The trouble with most books on computers is that they confuse computers, and what they can do, with the technology itself. The technology, what computers look like, what disks and keyboards look like, and how they work and so on is certainly both useful and fascinating, but these are not the issues raised in this book! An excellent introductory book to computers and what they mean is *Computer Science Unplugged: Off-line Activities and Games for All Ages*, by Tim Bell, Ian Witten and Mike Fellows. The activities are suitable for people of all ages and backgrounds and you don't need a computer to read the book. Full details of the book are available from its web site: http://unplugged.canterbury.ac.nz.

Cyberspace for Beginners, by Joanna Buick and Zoran Jevtic (Icon Books, 1999) is a useful introduction at a light-hearted level.

For a general introduction on what computers can and cannot do, see Douglas R. Hofstader's *Gödel, Escher, Bach: An Eternal Golden Braid* (Penguin, 1979). This is a classic book interleaving art, music, literature and computing, that could be recommended whole-heartedly to computer enthusiasts who want to get into something deeper. It is not an easy book.

On its fiftieth anniversary, the Association for Computing Machinery (the world's largest computer society) collected articles looking towards the future of computers. These articles are wide-ranging, and show a considerable concern for social issues. The message is: the scientific, social and economic impact of computers is only just beginning to be felt. *Beyond Calculation: The Next Fifty Years of Computing*, edited by Peter J. Denning and Robert Metcalf (Springer-Verlag, 1998).

Two books that contain short chapters covering a wide range of issues about IT and cyberspace are: *The Information Society: Evolving Landscapes*, edited by Jacques Berleur, Andrew Clement, R. Sizer and D. Whitehouse (Springer-Verlag, 1990) and *Computerization and Controversy; Value Conflicts and Social Choices*, edited by Charles Dunlop and Rob Kling (Academic Press, 1991).

For anyone considering practical issues of setting up a virtual community, reading up on the Blacksburg Electronic Village project is essential – this is the major wired local community in the United States. The book gives lots of food for thought and practical recommendations, technical and social. *Community Networks: Lessons from Blacksburg*, edited by Andrew M. Cohill and Andrea L. Kavanaugh (Artech House, 1997).

Is cyberspace new – or a continuation of previous development? One book that has been particularly illuminating is *Becoming Virtual: Reality in the Digital Age*, by Pierre Levy (Plenum, 1998). But be warned: this is written in the French philosophical tradition!

People responding to computer interaction as though it were reality – the so-called media equation – is an idea that is developed in *The Media Equation*, by Byron Reeves and Clifford Nass (Cambridge University Press, 1996).

Privacy and surveillance

The Christian sociologist David Lyon has written widely on the increasing surveillance of people as they go about their everyday lives, beginning in his *Silicon Society* (Lion Publishing, 1986) and continuing with *The Electronic Age: The Rise of the Surveillance Society* (Polity Press, 1994).

The Community Affairs Board of the Irish Council of Churches undertook a close look at the nature of privacy. Their small pamphlet, at times quite philosophical, but always readily accessible, is undated and highly recommended: *A Study on Privacy with Special Reference to Computers, Technical Surveillance and the Media.*

How do the new communications affect individuals? Sherry Turkel is a clinical psychologist, who examines what computers can do to our inner lives in *Life on the Screen: Identity in the Age of the Internet* (Weidenfeld & Nicolson, 1996).

Computing and its practice

A very good introduction to computer ethics in general is the short and clear textbook by Deborah Johnson, *Computer Ethics*, second edition (Prentice Hall, 1994).

A good primer on the Internet itself is Howard Rheingold's *The Virtual Community* (Minerva, 1995). This book emphasizes the human impact, and explains the new technological frontier and what it does for communities.

For how and why computers and communications work, and what they may achieve, building on Rheingold, and explaining why we're only just beginning, read *Being Digital*, by Nicholas Nigroponte (Coronet Books, 1995).

A good explanation of some of the new technical possibilities, particularly for business (electronic commerce), is Daniel C. Lynch and Leslie Lundquist's *Digital Money* (John Wiley, 1996). The book explains the new ideas of public key cryptography and applications, such as in writing cheques.

A detailed analysis of what might be considered professional for an information expert is found in *Ethics of Information Management*, edited by Richard O. Mason, Florence M. Mason and Mary J. Culnan (Sage, 1995).

Computers are very successful, we are told, but all is not well because they are hard to use – or, at least, they are harder to use than they need be. The classic analysis of the problem is Tom Landauer's book, which concludes that successful use of computers must be based in human needs: *The Trouble with Computers* (MIT Press, 1995).

Joseph Weizenbaum's *Computer Power and Human Reason* (Penguin Books, 1993), was the classic 'wake-up call' to computer experts to consider ethical issues, and raises 'objectively' many human issues that were being ignored.

Can computers think?

There is a vast literature on the computer, thinking and the brain, of which the most accessible in the Christian tradition is *God and the Mind Machine: Computers, Artificial Intelligence and the Human Soul*, by John Puddefoot (SPCK, 1996).

On how minds, brains and computers relate, see Philip Johnson-Laird, *The Computer and the Mind*, second edition (Fontana Press, 1993), and Roger Penrose with Abner Shimony, Nancy Cartwright and Stephen Hawking, *The Large, the Small and the Human Mind* (Cambridge University Press, 1997) (see, for example, Chapter 3, Physics and the Mind).

More to face than just being under lock and key . . .

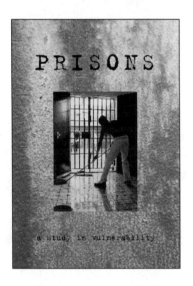

Prisons: A Study in Vulnerability

The last decade has seen a great many changes in the management of prisons, as well as a large increase in their population. One of the primary concerns, now at the heart of the prison debate in England, is the treatment of groups who are particularly vulnerable within the prison population; namely women, young people, those with a mental illness, minority ethnic groups and the families of prisoners. This collection of essays helps Christians consider the issue of vulnerability in the prison context, and also looks at prison chaplaincy and the theology of vulnerability.

Price £5.95

ISBN 0 7151 6584 4